Praise for
The Investor's Guide to Technical Analysis

"Curt Renz is well known as an outstanding on-air TV and Web site stock market analyst. His skillful interpretation of the market's technical underpinnings make for an understandable read for most market observers."

—Morris R. Beschloss
Editor, *The Beschloss Perspective*

"Sound technical analysis is a fundamental for successful investment. Technical analysis is also a very complicated task. Curt has done a wonderful job in turning the complicated concepts into easy-to-read language. It is a must read for investors who want to win the game in today's stock market."

—Charles C. Zhang, CFP, ChFC, CLU
The #1 Rated Financial Advisor in American Express in 2002

"In *The Investor's Guide to Technical Analysis*, Curt Renz has provided investors what they need to learn on their way to investment independence."

—Jim Welsh
Editor, *The Financial Commentator*
Principal, Welsh Money Management

"Curt Renz provides a clear introduction to technical analysis. It will prove useful not only to investors exploring technical analysis for the first time but also will be valuable to most other investors. The price history of a stock or index tells a story, and it is one which fundamental investors also need to understand as part of their decision-making process. Curt points out how different charts indicate the psychology of investors, which creates specific price patterns. These patterns will help alert investors to potential mistakes. Reading Curt's book will improve investors' investment decisions."

—Jim McCamant
Editor-at-Large, *Medical Technology Stock Letter*
Author, *Biotech Investing*

"Upon finishing Curt's book, I felt as if I could read the market's mind."
—Sam Stovall
Chief Investment Strategist
Standard & Poor's

"Curt has spent many years in the market information business, much of it simplifying technical subjects to those with less exposure to them. A solid read!"
—Arch Crawford
Editor, *Crawford Perspectives*

"At last, an investment book that is as entertaining as it is informative. With language and charts that are easily comprehensible, Curt Renz nimbly guides the reader through the arcane world of technical analysis."
—Jeffrey Schvimer
Director of Operations
Mesirow Financial Asset Management

"Curt has put together an excellent technical handbook for investors. It is an easy read and helps one to establish skills for successful investing. The section on charting is particularly helpful in defining some of the more potent formations for investing in the underlying trend."
—A. C. Moore
Chief Investment Strategist
Dunvegan Associates, Inc.

"The ability to balance fundamental and technical analysis is critical to the success of any investor's portfolio. With the increase of program trading and volatility in the markets that has occurred in the past few years, I sincerely believe that technical analysis is becoming a larger factor in the investment decision process today. Having read numerous books on technical analysis, I would say that Curt's ability to present one of the toughest subjects in informative and substantive chapters is a must read for anyone who has funds invested in the markets."
—Jim Collins, CFA
Chairman & CEO
Insight Capital Research & Management

"A great place to start for learning how to read stock charts."

—J. Michael Pinson
Founder, MarketMavens.com and
InvestmentBooks.com

"In addition to giving a good overview of technical analysis, Curt's book provides readers with practical, hands-on instruction and experience in correctly drawing trendlines and support-resistance levels for themselves, using graphs showing specific examples of common chart formations . . . most helpful, particularly for a novice or beginner unfamiliar with the subject."

—Kennedy Gammage
Editor and Publisher
The Richland Report

"Technical analysis is one of the few tried-and-true investment strategies an individual can learn to use and effectively apply at home with nothing more complex than paper and a pencil. Really. Curt Renz's book opens this world of chart formations and techniques to the average investor and to the novice investor. His book is accessible. It has a teaching approach. The examples and pointers are clear. Best of all, the book introduces something that works! Learn that 'head and shoulders' is not just a shampoo and that 'double bottoms' are not references to people with weight problems. Learn the lingo. Walk the walk, talk the talk—reap the gains. Renz's book is a winner. Use it to learn technical analysis, to manage your affairs, or to double-check your broker. It's your money . . . and some of it is well spent, I should say, invested, on this book."

—Robert A. Brusca, Ph.D.
Chief Economist
Native American Securities Co.

"Curt Renz's book on technical analysis will be a light in the dark for investors who have been hurt so badly over the past few years. Who knows? It could even light the way for so many of the professionals who have depended on fundamentals for their decision making and who have also been badly hurt doing so. It's a book that should benefit anyone with money in the stock market."

—Peter Eliades
Editor and Publisher
Stockmarket Cycles

"Curt Renz, from his unique perspective as a stock market commentator, has produced an excellent introduction to the perverse psychology of the stock market and describes the telltale price and volume behaviors that result. He introduces indicators that help identify general market trending and extreme conditions. Before and after worksheet charts invite readers to test their newly learned skills and check their analysis."

—Sherman McClellan
Publisher
McClellan Financial Publications, Inc.

"Curt Renz has written an invaluable primer on technical analysis, in clear and understandable language. His test exercise chapter by itself justifies the reader's interest. For investor's seeking to demystify the stock market, and substantially improve their probabilities for success, this book provides the basic tools."

—Donald D. Hahn, CFA
Chief Investment Strategist
Mesirow Financial Asset Management

"Curt has tackled one of the least understood techniques in investment decision making and done it in a manner that is easy to understand by the layperson. He provides clear explanations for such oddly named creatures such as 'head and shoulders formations' and 'double and triple tops.' Even fundamental investors who might not be prepared to base their investment actions on technical analysis as such would benefit from this exposure to another way of looking at the message of the market."

—Alfred F. Kugel
Senior Investment Strategist
Stein Roe Investment Counsel LLP

"Curt Renz makes sense of technical analysis. The book demonstrates how charts read the market's mind and illustrate investor behavior."

—Robert Gordon
President
Twenty-First Securities Corp.

"This is one of the best books on technical analysis available today. Everyone, and I mean everyone, looks at a chart before buying a stock. If you want to understand what many investors see in the chart patterns, this is the book for you."

—Mitch Zacks
Vice President
Zacks Investment Management

"An insightful, concise, witty, and easily understood primer for anyone wishing to get the 'inside scoop' on technical analysis—a job well done."

—Mark Leibovit, CIMA
VRTrader.com

"Finally, a book on technical analysis that is ideal for the private investor. Highly illuminating, without all the mathematical esoterica; it is remarkably easy to read and understand."

—Robert Morrow
President
Morrow Institutional Advisory

THE INVESTOR'S GUIDE TO TECHNICAL ANALYSIS

THE INVESTOR'S GUIDE TO TECHNICAL ANALYSIS

CURT RENZ

McGraw-Hill

New York   Chicago   San Francisco
Lisbon   London   Madrid   Mexico City
Milan   New Delhi   San Juan   Seoul
Singapore   Sydney   Toronto

4 5 6 7 8 9 0   FGR/FGR   0 9 8 7 6 5

ISBN 0-07-138998-9

This publication is designed to provide accurate and authoritative information in regard to the subject matter covered. It is sold with the understanding that neither the author nor the publisher is engaged in rendering legal, accounting, futures/securities trading, or other professional service. If legal advice or other expert assistance is required, the services of a competent professional person should be sought.

—From a Declaration of Principles jointly adopted by a Committee
of the American Bar Association and a Committee of Publishers

McGraw-Hill books are available at special quantity discounts to use as premiums and sales promotions, or for use in corporate training programs. For more information, please write to the Director of Special Sales, Professional Publishing, McGraw-Hill, Two Penn Plaza, New York, NY 10121-2298. Or contact your local bookstore.

This book is printed on recycled, acid-free paper containing a minimum of 50% recycled, de-inked fiber.

Library of Congress Cataloging-in-Publication Data

Renz, Curt.
   The investor's guide to technical analysis / by Curt Renz.
      p.   cm.
   ISBN 0-07-138998-9 (acid-free)
   1. Portfolio management.   2. Investment analysis.   I. Title.
HG4529.5.R46   2004
332.63'2042—dc21

                                                2003013190

To my mother, Betty Orth Mikkelsen, who departed our world during the preparation of this work. She was a brilliant and beautiful woman who devoted herself to properly raising four sons, of whom I was the eldest. Mom, you were to have received the first printed copy. Even though you will never see the book, I hope that others, by reading it, will detect the strength of character that you passed on to your grateful descendents.

CONTENTS

Part 3   PRACTICALITIES

PREFACE

2000

The Year of Dashed Dreams

Let's turn back the clock a few years to 2000, the year that had long signified a far distant future, a golden era in which all would turn out well. Indeed, all is well as the millennium begins. The world is at peace. That feared Y2K bug turned out to be harmless. The economy is booming as never before, thanks to that marvelous new Internet. And your stock portfolio has grown nicely. As you revel with friends on a beautiful New Year's Eve, you cannot resist bragging about what a clever stock picker you have been. The fact that they have similar stories hardly punctures your ego. It is a night for celebration, a time for all to be joyful.

Yes, that was the happy time. Making money without actually working for it had never been easier (and may never be again). All that you had to do was to buy a few dot-com stocks, then watch your portfolio expand. And expand, and expand, and expand. Something like blowing a bubble. Yes, exactly like blowing a bubble. You should have known what happens to bubbles. They burst, of course. And this one was no different. The pop was just a lot louder this time.

In the coming years, baby boomers will be retiring. When they were in their twenties and thirties, they bought homes and pushed up the price of real estate. When in their thirties and forties, they bought investments and pushed up share prices. As they retire, they'll be cashing in their shares and a less-populous generation will be doing the investing. That implies stagnancy in stock prices until the "echo" baby boom matures. Forget about leaving your money in an index mutual fund and counting on significant growth. Those who will be making real money in the stock market in the coming years will be those who learn how the game is played and take control of their own investments. That means studying the companies in which you plan to invest and learning how to read their charts. If you're not willing to do that, then stick with fixed-income investments.

Is it possible for you and everyone else to make money without actually working? Of course not! Somebody has to produce the goods and services on which you would like to spend that money. For a while, though, during the late nineties, it certainly seemed possible. But that was an illusion. The bubble burst, and all of its riders fell down. That is, except for a few who were aware of the lessons of history. Lessons that can be learned by studying the patterns of the past and applying them to the present. Those patterns are often seen in the charts of stock prices and trading volumes. But learning and applying those lessons requires a little work. You now know that. And that is why you bought this book.

Curt Renz

INTRODUCTION

What's in This for Me?

A Better Way to Time Your Trades

This book will show you how to read the market's mind. No, not in the psychic sense. But we are all able to estimate what others must be thinking, even without their speaking. From their actions and their body language we gather clues. And, surprisingly, often our inferences are correct.

In the marketplace, people speak with their money. Often a person or a group of people has reason to buy shares of stock, but does not express that reason publicly. Significant buying, though, does show up in the daily trading volume. And that buying interest can boost the price of the shares. These price and volume movements signal to the alert investor that somebody knows something. But whatever that something is may not yet be in the news. Perhaps they are customers or suppliers of a company. They may sense that business is picking up for that firm. The next quarterly report may verify this. But those who suspect that business has improved will not wait for that verification before making stock purchases. The buyers may not be sharing their insights, but their interest in the company is evident in the price and volume action of the stock.

If you understand the art of stock market technical analysis, you may be able to match the recent trading in a stock with similar patterns that have been repeated many times in the past. Then you can take action, buying or selling as appropriate. Would your analysis make the trade a sure thing? Certainly not. Your analysis may have been faulty. An unusual factor may have been overlooked. An event expected by no one may occur. But the probabilities should be in your favor if you have really done your homework.

Even if you do not learn to apply the sections of this book directly related to technical analysis, you should benefit greatly from the early chapters that point out how investors usually go wrong. And most investors do indeed do the wrong thing at the wrong time. They buy when everyone is excited about the market and pushing prices to ridiculous extremes, extremes that are unsustainable. They sell when everyone is frustrated with the market and bailing out at bargain basement prices. In this book, you will learn when it may actually be wise to run with the crowd and when it may be smarter to take advantage of the folly of others.

The early chapters of this book explain how markets operate and stock prices are determined. Those who are fully aware of the price-setting mechanism can skip over this material. But far too many others really have no idea how stock market prices are set. Too many assume that some folks on Wall Street serve the same function as the management at a supermarket chain. No, Wall Street does not simply mark prices that you are forced to accept. I'll show you how it really works.

A little later, you will learn how various cycles of activity also regulate the habits of investors. These cycles can influence stock prices. You will learn a simple technique for lazy investors that might allow you to stay ahead of the market by making trades only 2 days a year.

You will also be learning what kind of information you need to get in order to make rational decisions. All too often, investment decisions are the result of emotional reactions to the current market situation. Fear and greed have destroyed far too many investment portfolios.

You will learn that price action alone is often not sufficient to draw correct inferences. Volume, the number of shares being traded, can indicate whether a price move is for real or a fluke.

You will come to understand that the fundamental factors used in determining stock value usually are transmitted to you at a time too late for you to profit. The fundamentals also ignore the psychological factors that can predominate in the short and intermediate terms.

Much of the book will be devoted to the basic technical patterns that often foretell future market movement. This book is a primer for those new to technical analysis, therefore it will not go into complex patterns that are rarely seen. If you're seeking to obtain a job on Wall Street as a technical analyst, then you may want to follow up by reading a text that goes deeper. One of the best is the classic *Technical Analysis of Stock Trends* by Robert D. Edwards and John Magee. But the patterns described here should cover 95 percent of the situations that you might encounter.

Toward the end of the book, we will discuss ways to apply what you have learned to mutual fund switching and individual stock selection. It is highly recommended that you test your abilities as a technical analyst on paper before you step in with real money. Even then, you will not always be right. If you find your analysis is incorrect more often than not, then technical analysis may not be your forte. Perhaps you should stick to money market funds. But for those who become adept, the process will seem almost intuitive. Chapter 14 will attempt to help you to reach that point.

At the end of the book, you will find a series of test charts. They are similar to the charts you came across earlier, but clues such as support and resistance lines have not been drawn. It will be your job to draw them. It will be your job to forecast the future market direction. If you do well on the tests, congratulate yourself. But if you do not score 100, keep going back until you do. If you have not perfected your skill with the basic charts, then you are not ready to put real money at risk based on your analyses of real-world charts.

No matter how good a market technician this book helps you to become, it will make you a more knowledgeable investor who invests wisely with the head, rather than emotionally with the heart.

THE INVESTOR'S GUIDE TO TECHNICAL ANALYSIS

1

Basics

1

HOW STOCK PRICES ARE SET

Not the Way It's Done at the Grocery Store

TRADING PLACES
Where the Gods of Pricing Reside

You are watching a stock ticker roll by on financial television. And you wonder to yourself, "Are those buys or sells?" Many people ask that question. I know that they do. My television viewers ask me over the phone or by e-mail. And in response I ask, "Can there be a buyer without a seller?" Then comes a short pause as it dawns on the caller that the price crossing the ticker represents both a buy and a sell. It is, of course, a trade—the consummation of a deal transferring partial ownership of a company at an agreed-upon price between a buyer and a seller. The company itself is not normally one of those parties.

How did the buyer and seller get together? They didn't just meet on the street. Neither of them put out advertisements or made cold calls until someone responded to the offer. But they did make use of intermediaries who brought the two of them together. The central intermediary is the stock exchange. The exchange can be located in a large room, as at the New York Stock Exchange (NYSE), where representatives of the buyer and seller can strike a deal. Or it can be electronic, as with the National Association of Securities Dealers Automated Quotations (Nasdaq), where a computer matches individuals who have compatible price requirements.

But you say that you never stated a price requirement. You just told your broker to buy or sell. Of course, the broker is an extra layer between you and the exchange. That broker could have been a real person with whom you actually spoke, or the broker's computer that accepted your order over the Internet. If you failed to state your price, then you entered the order "at market." That meant that if you were buying, you were willing to pay the lowest price that any seller was asking. And if you were selling, you were willing to accept the highest price that anyone was bidding.

Who are the people doing the bidding and asking? It could be the specialist in your stock on the NYSE, who has agreed to step in, if he or she can't find anyone else to match your order. It could be a market maker in your stock on the Nasdaq, who always provides both a bid to buy and an offer (asking price) to sell. And it could be someone like you who has given the broker a limit price.

If you were buying, that limit would be the highest price you were willing to pay. If that price were higher than anyone else's, it would become the *inside bid*. If you were selling, that limit would be the lowest price you were willing to accept. And if that price were lower than anyone else's, it would become the *inside offer* (or *ask*).

If yours is the inside bid or offer, it becomes the first one executed with another party who is willing to accept the market price.

So the prices of shares trading on the various exchanges are not arbitrarily pegged by some overseer in the way that groceries are priced in a supermarket. They are not set by an analyst who has assessed a company's financial statements to determine fair value. Stocks are sold in a two-way auction market in which prices are determined by competing bids and offers.

As we have learned, these people can be anybody. They can be people who know next to nothing about a particular company. Perhaps they are just following the advice of a broker or a tip from a friend. They can be corporate insiders who know a great deal, or those on the fringe in possession of a specific piece of information. They can be those caught up in a frenzy of greed or fear. Or they can be those who have been following the price and volume data of a stock and infer from the patterns what those others must be thinking or planning. The final group is the clever type into which I intend to transform you.

ECON 101
What Supply and Demand Really Mean

You call your broker to ask why your stock dropped a couple of dollars today. She answers, "More sellers than buyers." She could find no news on the company, so she falls back on this standard cliché. You quickly get off the phone realizing that you are not going to learn much from her. Then you pause and think. How can there be more sellers than buyers? As we just learned, every trade involves both a buyer and a seller. Yes, a buyer can buy from more than one seller, and a seller can sell to more than one buyer. But that all averages out over the course of the day. In any event, the number of shares bought or sold must be precisely equal. So what was your broker trying to tell you? The broker meant that today there were more people willing to sell at yesterday's closing price than those who were willing to buy at that price. To equalize their numbers, the sellers had to lower their expectations and accept lower prices if deals were to be done.

On a happier day that same broker may tell you that there were more buyers than sellers. In that case she would actually have meant that today more people were willing to buy at yesterday's closing price than were willing to sell at that price. And to equalize their numbers, the buyers had to become more aggressive and pay higher prices, if deals were to be done.

So how does this relate to the concept of *supply and demand*? Today's potential sellers own the supply of shares available for sale near the current price. The potential buyers are those demanding to become owners near the current price.

Figure 1-1 is like many that you will find in a standard introductory economics textbook. The vertical axis shows possible prices for a share of a stock. The horizontal axis indicates the number of shares that buyers might buy or sellers might sell. Our primary interest is in the two curves drawn on the chart. The darker up-sloping line is the *supply curve*. The lighter down-sloping line is the *demand*

FIGURE 1-1

Supply and Demand I

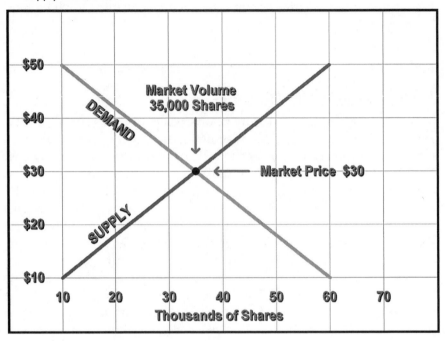

curve. In actuality, the lines really do curve, but we'll keep things simple here.

The supply curve tells how many shares would be willingly sold at any specific price level. Notice that at higher prices more shares are offered. The demand curve tells us how many shares would be willingly bought at each of those price levels. Only at lower prices are more shares demanded.

Focus on the point where those two curves cross. They cross at the equilibrium price level at which equal numbers of shares would be willingly bought or sold. And that graphically points to today's theoretical market price and volume.

Now let's suppose that more sellers enter the market. We can illustrate this new situation by shifting the supply curve to the right as in Figure 1-2. Notice that the new equilibrium level is at a lower price but has greater volume than in Figure 1-1.This is just what you might expect with an increase in supply.

FIGURE 1-2

Supply and Demand II

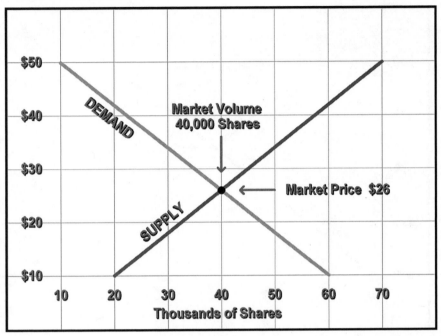

On the other hand, what if more buyers enter the market? To demonstrate this case we would shift the demand curve to the right as in Figure 1-3. This new equilibrium is at a higher price and also has greater volume than in Figure 1-1. That should be no surprise.

Of course, if the number of sellers or buyers were instead reduced, then the supply or demand curve would be shifted to the left. In either case, the volume would drop. If the sellers dwindled, then prices would rise. This is illustrated by going from Figure 1-2 back to Figure 1-1. If the buyers dried up, then prices would fall. To see this pictured, go from Figure 1-3 back to Figure 1-1.

Figures 1-1, 1-2, and 1-3 illustrate graphically how it is that a large number of interacting participants with diverse interests together determine market price and volume. It is the system resulting from the actions of these many people that we call the *market*. The market, therefore, is not a singular authority figure dictating prices. It is all of us, each acting in his or her own self-interest.

FIGURE 1-3

Supply and Demand III

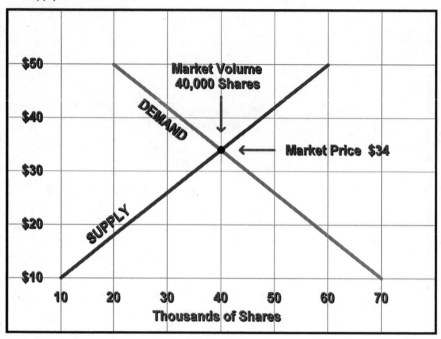

Eighteenth-century economist Adam Smith likened the market to an invisible hand creating order out of seeming chaos. But he knew as we do that that is only a simple analogy. The reality is more complex, but its basics can be grasped by those of us with quite visible hands. Understanding how the system really works puts us far ahead of our competitors in the market place.

FEAR AND GREED

They'll Get You Every Time

Of course you are a rational investor. Emotions play no part in your investing decisions. It's all of those other silly people who can be overcome with fear or enticed by greed. If only that were true. But these emotions were wired into the brains of our ancestors long before they developed the ability to reason. And you and I still have them. They are centered in a lower portion of the brain call the

R-complex. R stands for reptilian. It represents the highest level of brain development for reptiles. But we mammals have overlain this region with a neocortex. This includes the reasoning portion of the brain. The neocortex can overrule the signals from the R-complex. At times, however, the emotions are just too powerful to be overcome. Often that's for the good, as when our ancestors were confronted with threats to their lives. But it's rarely for your good when making investment decisions.

Fear induced our ancestors to flee an unpleasant situation without the need to take the time to reason through the situation. Taking too much time could mean becoming lunch for a growling predator. Eventually, people figured out ways to make weapons with which they could slay their enemies. Now, with spear in hand when confronted by a savage beast, a human being's rational brain could take a moment to overrule the emotions and send a missile flying to end that particular threat permanently.

Greed caused our ancestors to consume a greater share of a downed beast than was immediately necessary. This emotion was developed both to build up fat reserves for leaner times and to show dominance over other members of the group. Later, people reasoned that the storing and trading of surpluses, as well as cooperation with others in the group, were of greater benefit to the community than individual greed.

These emotions of fear and greed can also become infectious. We know how silly gossip caused fear to run rampant in Salem, Massachusetts, during the late seventeenth century. Salem was an educated community, taught much about the workings of nature by Isaac Newton and other scientists earlier in the century. But fear for their immortal souls caused these otherwise rational people to pursue a tragic witch hunt.

Much earlier in the seventeenth century, tulips had been imported to Holland from the East. Tulip gardens were much in demand, and many would pay any price to have one. As people bid against one another for the modest supply of tulip bulbs, single bulbs eventually traded for the price of an entire farm. Of course, tulips do have the ability to reproduce. Soon the country became a sea of tulips. If you understood the concept of supply and demand discussed earlier, you know what happened next. The cost of tulips plummeted, and some poor farmers had no farms, only a single lovely tulip to contemplate.

The tulip bubble was classic. There have been many other bubbles that have burst since then. You weren't expecting people to learn from past mistakes, were you? Our emotions will remain with us for countless more generations and will continue to influence our investment decisions, both individually and as members of a crowd.

Naturally, when most of the economic news gets bad, investors become fearful and refrain from putting their money into the stock market. Those already in the market become eager to get out. The supply of available shares gets bigger while the demand dissipates. Prices plunge. As prices spiral downward, more investors wave the white flag and dump their shares. Eventually this process gets out of control. People should realize that times always get better and that most corporations soon will resume generating a nice stream of income. Nevertheless, the market has become oversold with share prices far below reasonable values because of a wave of hysteria.

Later we enter a time of plenty. Technological innovations such as the Internet create a more productive economy. The talk in the air is of a "new era," in which the business cycle has been abolished. The stock market has been booming for quite a while, and many who got out of the market at its last bottom now feel it's time to get back in. Why not? Everyone else is doing it, and some have made quite a bit of money. Another initial public offering (IPO) for a company's shares comes out, and you have to have some. Why take the time to learn who runs the firm and what they intend to do with your money? The name ends in dot-com; that's all you need to know. Of course, everyone should have realized that the picture could not be as rosy as had been painted. Not all of these new competing firms are going to be successful. The market has become overbought with share prices pushed far above reasonable values as everyone squeezes on board.

Of course, someone is buying *from* those anxious sellers during a market panic, and someone is selling *to* those excited buyers during a market bubble. Are they stupid? Sometimes they are. They may be people who were burned during an earlier market cycle and are determined to behave in a contrary manner. But if they haven't really done their homework, they may make their moves far too early. This is where sound technical analysis comes in. The archetypal technical patterns of price and volume have been gleaned from hard-learned historical examples. They give strong clues as to what is underlying the market and where it will likely be going. Those who buy near market bottoms and sell near market tops are known as the "smart money," those with "strong hands." When a market seems to be bottoming and these wise ones start buying, the market is said to be in "accumulation." As a market appears to be peaking and they start selling, the market is said to be under "distribution."

Have you been running with the "dumb money," the "weak hands" who get shortchanged every time? Then read on. Follow the principles in this book and before long you may be riding in style with the pros.

2

CYCLES

The Lessons of History

CREATURES OF HABIT

Hearing the Rhythmic Beat

Cycles are evident throughout nature and in our daily lives. The sun rises and sets. The seasons turn with a seemingly unending and predictable pattern. Much longer term, ice ages ebb and flow as the earth's orbit and orientation fluctuate at a pace conforming to the laws of physics.

Many of these natural patterns have influenced the development of genes that regulate behavior in plants and animals. The daily cycle is the most obvious. Many animals are only active when the sun is up and seeing is good. Birds and insects will seek out the nectar offered by flowering plants, which only open their petals during the hours when flying creatures will visit and help transfer pollen. As the seasons progress, trees sprout and then shed their leaves. Birds migrate. Young animals are generally born in the spring to allow them time to ready themselves for the next winter. And all living things go through entire life cycles that are then repeated by their progeny.

Some cycles are more systemic, affecting more than one species over a period of several years. In an area lush with plant life and

FIGURE 2-1

Ecological Cycles

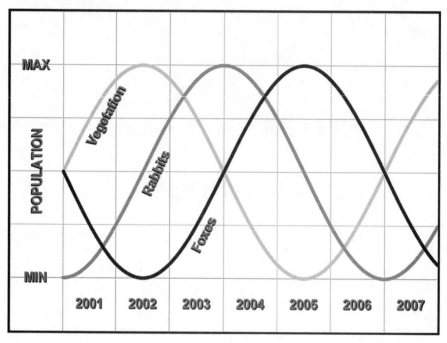

few predators, a population of rabbits may grow rapidly. Then the fox population will grow in response to plentiful prey. Eventually, this large congregation of rabbits will defoliate the vegetation. The combination of fewer plants and more foxes causes the rabbit population to crash. In turn, the foxes will die off. And with a shortage of rabbits, the vegetation will again become lush, setting up the ecology for the beginning of another cycle. (See Figure 2-1.)

Cycles analogous to the natural ones are evident in the stock market. Of course, these cycles are not really unnatural. Human beings are a part of the natural world and their behavioral genes remain evident as we learned in Chapter 1. We see daily patterns in the market as nonprofessionals tend to place their orders early, while the pros wait until they have learned more later in the day. We see weekly behavior as mergers are announced on Mondays and traders close out positions on Fridays. We see monthly patterns because of the increased flow of pension fund money early in the month and then options expiration later. The Federal Open Market Committee (FOMC) meets every 6 or 7 weeks to determine monetary policy. Quarterly, we come into earnings report season. Annual cycles can be influenced by tax considerations and distracted attention during the summer months. Economic data are released in cycles of varying lengths. Presidential elections are held quadrennially and greatly affect fiscal policy.

Although these varying cycles do influence the fundamentals that underlie the stock market, the actual movement of the market may seem to be out of sync. Most new participants expect the market to be in lockstep with the economy. Wouldn't it be nice if we could time the market just by staying up to date on the economic releases? Instead, stock prices usually turn long before the economy does. Some market players sense changes in the prospects for certain companies or industries well before the economic data come out and make their investments accordingly. Thus, prices will change before the reasons are publicly known.

With millions of participants in the economy and the stock market, the interplay can be quite complex. Consider that interaction among the fox, the rabbit, and the vegetation multiplied countless times. As one of my business management professors taught, everything depends on everything else. Even so, as with that simple ecology, the system of interplay among the various actors in the economy can lead to repeatable cycles. Those with knowledge of these cycles and the confidence that they will endure have taken the first step that places them ahead of others who are trying to outguess the market. In later chapters we will investigate these cycles of varying length and eventually integrate them with the technical analysis of stock prices and trading volume.

THE CICADA RETURNS
Why Long-Term Cycles Endure

In 1956 the cicada returned to the Midwest. They are popularly known as the 17-year locust. Therefore, the infestation was no surprise since they previously made an appearance in 1939. Of course, they came again in 1973 and 1990. Count on them in 2007. Why do the cicada behave this way? The pattern evolved in their genes over millions of generations. For this particular species, it was proven that they could avoid predators and conserve resources by hiding as eggs for nearly 17 years.

In human affairs, some see a civilization cycle of many centuries. In Europe, during the first millennium before Christ, most people were nature worshippers who held their priestly caste in high esteem. At some point, though, a combination of disagreeable climate change, plague, and pestilence forced some villages to discover the advantages of banding together in hard times. Trading of goods and ideas increased exponentially. Civilization spread, eventually leading to the secular world of the mighty Roman Empire. The enhanced economic productivity supported a city of a million inhabitants.

Centuries later the barbarian tribes to the north moved in, toppled the empire, and set up the feudal society of the Middle Ages. The economy collapsed into a dark age in which no city could claim a population of as much as 100,000. People once again turned to the priestly caste for solace. By the late Middle Ages, however, the middle class of craftsmen, artisans, merchants, and teachers waxed in political power. Cities grew and universities were founded. This rebirth of learning and culture, the Renaissance, led to the rise of a new secular civilization. Trade again flourished. Scientific discoveries produced technological innovations and an industrial revolution. City-states unified into the economically powerful nation-states we see today.

Whether Western civilization is now at an important turning point remains to be seen. The tendency is for people to believe that life will go on as it always has. But for most people that means "as it has been during their lives and those of their parents and grandparents." If we stand back and look at the sweep of history over the millennia, we know that this is not the case. And very-long-term cyclical patterns become evident.

Other long-term cycles, though not of millennial degree, have been noted by some academicians, such as the early twentieth-century Russian economist, Kondratieff. He saw an approximately 60-year cycle during which economic activity alternated between good and hard times. His theory may need some reworking, since the Depression of the 1930s certainly did not reappear in the 1990s. If we accept that 70 years is approximately 60 years, then we might note that the stock market began a crash in late 1929 and again in early 2000 (1987 was barely a blip). Great advances in technology, mostly related to electricity, preceded the Crash of 1929. The ubiquitous computer and its child, the Internet, pumped up the bubble that burst in 2000. In both cases, we were indeed entering new eras. Many investors believed that this meant price was no object when buying shares of companies in these pioneering industries. They were rudely awakened.

There exists in the United States a 4-year cycle. As this country grew and the central government took on a greater role in economic activity through its fiscal policy, the 4-year presidential election cycle began to influence the business cycle. The party in power tends to restrain the budget during the early years after an election, often because it promised to cut taxes if elected. This reduction in government spending leads to an economic slowdown. When things really get bad the Federal Reserve enters the picture by lowering interest rates as a stimulus to economic activity.

Then, as the next election approaches, the administration desperately requests that Congress dole from the Treasury whatever various constituencies demand. After the government has been spending heavily for a while, business booms since much of this money, directly or indirectly, ends up in corporate treasuries. When a point is reached at which industry can no longer produce at the pace demanded by those with dollars, inflation ensues as people bid up the price of what is available. The Federal Reserve then steps in to raise interest rates in hopes of cooling off the inflation. It usually does this late in an election cycle. Why not? The Federal Reserve is not running for anything. Later, after a new administration has moved into the White House demanding fiscal restraint, everyone is then surprised by a slowing economy, and the whole cycle begins again.

We have examined long-term cycles of varying lengths. The centuries-long cycles of civilization may not be useful to an individual with a limited life span. The Kondratieff cycle may remind folks that new technological eras can actually create market bubbles, not eliminate them. Don't stay too long with the mania when the next one occurs. Although, you are probably too old to ever see another. The presidential cycle and its companion business cycle may be quite useful for determining overall investment allocation over a period of a couple of years. Always be aware of what Washington is up to; politicians can affect much more of your financial situation than just your taxes. They can influence the prices of your stock shares.

THE INCONSTANT MOON
Repetitive Short-Term Events

For many people reading this book, the long-term cycles just discussed are of little concern. These people may not hold stock positions for as long as a year. For some, a week may be a long hold. Indeed, there are regular cycles of which even these traders must be aware.

Early human beings surely anticipated the daily rising and setting of the sun. They were undoubtedly aware of the annual cycle of seasons. But our earliest ancestors lived in the tropics where the seasonal effects are not as pronounced as in temperate zones. Interestingly, we have evidence that some wise folks followed the monthly cycle of lunar phases. Anthropologists have found 30,000-year-old carvings in bone that appear to be depictions of the waxing and waning of the moon. Counting to 365 may have been beyond the skill level of these ancient people, but marking off the six full moons of the dry season and the six full moons of the wet season may not have been so difficult. The modern month, though, is somewhat artificial since the moon actually averages about 12.37 phase cycles in a year, not 12.00. Of course, in more recent millennia, human society has developed the artifice of a 7-day-week, which now plays a more prominent role in our lives than does the month.

THE DAILY GRIND

All of the aforementioned time frames help to regulate activity in the economy and the stock market. Our days are regulated by a clock that simulates the apparent motion of the sun through the heavens. Our employers expect us to be at work at a prescribed time and not to leave until a stated hour. For most of us, these hours are during daylight. The stock market follows the same plan.

Most nonprofessional investors are busy at work while the stock market is open. When they get home in the evening, they learn of the day's market events from television. Or perhaps they catch up the following morning with a financial newspaper. They tend to make decisions during this period when the market is resting. They place their orders with their brokers before leaving for work or shortly after arriving. Then they just hope for the best.

Professional money managers, however, have the luxury of being able to follow the market while it is open. They can easily place orders at any moment of the market day. They tend to bide their time, digest the news, observe the actions of others, and then make their commitments.

You might now be able to recognize the origin of the old Wall Street adage, "The dumb money makes its moves in the morning, while the smart money acts in the afternoon." When you see the market sell off in the morning, don't panic. The pros don't. They take the time to assess the situation, and, if the morning sell-off appears unwarranted, they swoop in later to pick up bargains. Conversely, if buyers are predominant in the morning, the pros often eagerly take profits in the afternoon.

If you are a member of the crowd that places market orders before the opening, get out of it. If you are subject to a margin call, don't wait for your broker to forcibly liquidate your position at the market opening.

Make your trades during a less frenzied time of the day. That's what the pros do.

WEEKS AND MONTHS

Weekly events play a role in the market. Expect mergers to be announced before the market opens on Mondays.

The negotiators find it is easier to discuss and finalize deals in secret during a weekend. If you are expecting a company to be bought out at a premium, then consider making your move late in the week. Otherwise, on Monday you'll find yourself saying, "I knew it; I should have done something." Remember, you can never "should have." You cannot go back in time.

Traders often get out of positions before a weekend, especially before long holiday weekends. If the market sells off on a Thursday and then stabilizes Friday morning, expect many short-sellers to cover their positions (buy) in the afternoon. Conversely, if the market rallies on Thursday with little follow-through on Friday morning, look for traders who are long to bail out later in the day.

The monthly calendar should also be studied. It's chock full of repetitively scheduled economic data. We'll be discussing how to use this information to your benefit in the next chapter.

On the first of the month, many pension fund managers receive fresh funds to put to work. That creates a demand for stocks that usually kicks off the month with an up day in the market. The previous day is usually up too, because of those who anticipate the buying on the first. In fact, the first 3 or 4 days of the month show an upward bias as those pension managers usually need a few days to establish new positions. This period gets a further boost from Social Security pensioners who receive their checks on the third of the month.

Once we get toward the middle of the month, the market anticipates options expiration. The last day for regular market dealing in these exchange-traded options is the third Friday of the month (that is, the Friday that falls on the fifteenth through the twenty-first). That formula was prescribed by the Chicago Board Options Exchange to minimize the possibility of the expiration falling on a holiday. Rarely, Good Friday falls on the prescribed date and the de facto expiration occurs on Thursday.

Arbitrageurs own hedge positions. They may own a basket of stocks, while having short calls or long puts on them. Or they may be short the stocks and hedge them the opposite way with options. As the options expiration date nears, they have a decision to make. They can close out all their positions, or they can close only the options and renew them for a later month: a rollover. Back in the 1980s this made for a nerve-wracking final hour on expiration Friday, known as the "witching hour." After the Crash of 1987, many of these "arbs" came to a tacit agreement with the exchanges to try to square up their positions during the middle of the week prior to the expiration. This has led to relatively volatile Wednesdays, which we Chicagoans know as "position squaring day." East Coast commentators are often baffled on that day and try to come up with varying explanations for what is going on. We know. Sharp day traders may be able to take advantage of this volatility. I would not advise anyone else to try.

Is options expiration week usually a good one or a bad one for the market? That depends on where we are in the quarter. Those that come in the middle months of a quarter (February, May, August, and November) show no unusual tendencies. But those that fall during the other months often demonstrate an upward bias. The actual expiration day usually mimics the rest of the week.

THE FED

Eight times per year (twice per quarter) the Federal Open Market Committee of the United States Federal Reserve Bank meets to determine monetary policy. I don't know if there is a connection, but they seem to schedule these meetings around the dates of the ancient European holidays (that is, the equinoxes, solstices, and celebrations that were midway between). Perhaps this gets them more in tune with nature. We won't get into the intricacies of their discussions here. Suffice it to say that they have control over certain short-term interest rates, and this can greatly affect the supply and movement of money. This in turn affects the economy and the stock market. Those who are good at guessing what the FOMC will do stand to profit.

EARNINGS SEASON

Quarterly, we come to earnings report season. Most companies, but hardly all, have fiscal quarters that coincide with the calendar quarters. Most of them report on their results during the second half of the month that begins the new quarter. This often leads to large moves for some stocks on the day following the release of their earnings news. Traders who guess right can be handsomely rewarded. Others may take substantial losses. Technical analysis can often give clues as to whether a company will surprise us positively or disappoint. We'll discuss this later in the book. Those who are not adept or are conservative by nature should stay away from this game. They would be better served by waiting to buy a stock until after they have seen its earnings report.

THE SIMPLEST RULE OF ALL

Are there annual cycles? Of course! The simplest no-brainer rule is to be in the market during the coldest half of the year and out during the warmest half. These periods are roughly delineated by April 20 and October 20. Tax dates play a role in making this work, as do maturation dates for bank certificates of deposit. Perhaps overriding the other considerations is the tendency of folks to become distracted during the summer. Market focus seems to return with the first frost.

Are the tendencies discussed in this chapter and the preceding one inviolable? Of course not! But in the long run knowledge of them may play to your advantage.

3

INDICATORS

Pointing the Way

MINING THE DATA
Getting to It before the Crowd

Almost every day market participants are inundated with economic data from the government and private sources. Much of this is macro-economic information on matters ranging from consumer sentiment to factory usage. A lot more is in the form of announcements from individual companies, especially earnings reports. The majority of these data are released outside of market hours to give participants time to mull over all of the supporting statistics and comments.

When news is released during regular trading hours, some traders will react quickly to the headline and then experience remorse as the full text is revealed. This can even happen after regular hours for those who trade at that time. For instance, the first line crossing the wires may state that a company earned two cents per share better than expected for the previous quarter. Some traders with a quick trigger finger will buy immediately, hoping to beat the crowd. The stock price takes a quick jump. Then a minute later comes an indication that expectations for the current quarter are now much less than previously estimated. And the stock price immediately sinks to much lower levels.

It is almost always known in advance when macroeconomic data and corporate earnings reports will be released. The wild cards are earnings preannouncements in which companies will confess that the quarter is looking poor (occasionally the opposite) some weeks before the quarter ends. They supposedly do this to eliminate surprises, especially negative ones, on the day that the earnings are actually released. Senior corporate officers feel they are less likely to be scrutinized by shareholders if the bad news comes out a little earlier. The pace of these announcements has greatly increased since the Securities and Exchange Commission (SEC) formulated Regulation FD (Fair Disclosure) in late 2000. Reg FD requires corporations to release material information to everyone all at the same time rather than to feed it individually to Wall Street analysts who ask for it. The result is that companies now keep information pent up until they suddenly decide to release it to the media. Since these announcements are not normally scheduled in advance, their surprise release can lead to huge moves in share prices, much greater than on the day of the official earnings report.

A STEP AHEAD

How then can you get a clue about what's going on before data are actually released? A difficult but effective way is to collect anecdotal evidence. If there is a good hard-working economist at your workplace, he or she can aid you in this busywork. If he's someone who simply goes along with the consensus, then he's less than useless. If you are considering investing in a particular company or industry, then learn from customers and suppliers of these companies. They know what the pace of the business is. That's what good analysts have to do in this world of Reg FD. Actually, the good ones always have, but others simply relied on data fed to them from senior corporate officers. Not anymore.

Corporate officers, directors, and large shareholders can trade their shares so long as they report the trade to the SEC. But simply knowing who is buying or selling is not enough. Insiders often sell to finance a major personal purchase, such as a home. The Web site *ThomsonFN.com* does a marvelous job of collecting the raw SEC data and assigning scores to corporate insiders for their abilities to time the market (that is, high marks if they buy before their stock moves up or sell before it moves down). Check it out.

There's another method for reading the tea leaves. It involves less work but requires the development of a new skill. That skill is the art of technical analysis. By following the patterns of stock price and volume, you can infer that something is going on at a particular company. The knowledgeable people mentioned in previous paragraphs will be buying or selling in accordance with what they know. They may not be talking with their lips, but what they do with their money speaks volumes. By following the charts you'll know when something good or bad is happening. You may not be able to infer exactly what that is. However, you will occasionally put two and two together and come up with the correct answer. But the reason for the stock activity really does not matter. So long as you can deduce from the chart which way the stock is headed, that is all you need to know. Technical analysis is far from perfect, but if properly used it should give you an advantage more often than not.

SENTIMENTAL JOURNEY
Why Everyone Gathers on the Wrong Side of the Boat

On Saturday, July 24, 1915, the Great Lakes cruise ship *Eastland* was loading Western Electric employees at a dock on the Chicago River for a short trip along the southern tip of Lake Michigan to a company picnic site. Everyone was eager to get together with friends. People began congregating on deck. The boat was notoriously unstable, and when too many passengers assembled toward the port side, the boat capsized. More than 800 lost their lives.

In the market we find investors placing themselves on the same side of the boat as everyone else. This applies to professional money managers as well as the public. The resulting disaster may not be as tragic as what happened to the people aboard the *Eastland*, but financially it can be devastating.

This tendency for investors to cluster together should not be surprising. People take comfort in doing the same as others. They get lulled into a false sense of security as they mimic the others' behavior. They tend to listen only to those whose opinions agree with their own. They will tune out those few who present a contrary point of view. At market bottoms they want to hear that they were right to sell out. At market tops they want to hear that they were not the "greater fool" who bought at top dollar. This makes it tough for a television commentator such as myself to call a market turn and still be loved.

The more obvious the case for a turn in the market to a good technician, the less obvious it is to the majority of investors. At such times I will exude confidence in my opinion, yet a large portion of my television audience will think that I am ridiculing them. Yet if I were to state the case in more sedate terms, they would doubt my certainty. I suppose that if I were a demagogue who really wanted his TV ratings to zoom, I would simply tell folks want they want to hear: They did the right thing and the market will keep moving in their direction. That may be soothing to them and make me more lovable, but it would be doing them a great disservice.

Normally, herding is the safe thing to do. It is right for prey animals. But in the market it causes prices to reach extremes. Those prices can be quite irrational. Our human experience with markets has been far too short for such behavior to have been weeded out by natural selection. On time scales more familiar to us, huge numbers of disillusioned investors will remove themselves from the market after a long decline. That can lead to protracted bear markets or markets that make no net progress over a considerable period of time. The period from 1966 to 1982 is the archetype for this behavior.

Is it always wrong to go with the crowd? Certainly not. From October 1999 to March 2000 the Nasdaq nearly doubled. Even at the beginning of that period, stocks were overvalued. But you missed out if you failed to stay with the trend until it peaked. However, at that peak investors were at their most bullish. And that was the time for them to set aside their greed, part with the herd, and get out. How would they have known when that point was reached? That will be covered when we get to technical analysis.

RATIONAL BEHAVIOR

Simple Division

When applying fundamental analysis, ratios are seen everywhere. Most of them result from the simple division of one number by another. The most well known is the *price-earnings ratio* or P/E. This is simply the current price of the stock divided by the earnings per share. Of course, the *earnings per share* (EPS) is also a ratio: the total earnings divided by the number of shares outstanding. Earnings (profits) are basically a company's income minus expenses. An entire book could be written about these fundamental ratios. In fact, many have been. Just check out the finance section of any college bookstore.

In this chapter, though, we will be looking at ratios that are more of interest to a technical analyst. Some will give us an idea of investor sentiment in the marketplace. Others will tell us where the momentum is now and where it may be headed.

SENTIMENT INDICATORS

Many of the ratios that a technician follows are related to market sentiment. If an unusually large number of market newsletter writers are bullish, the implication is that their subscribers are heavily invested in stocks. They may have depleted their cash reserves, leaving them with little buying power. They can cheer for the market to move up all they want, but that will do no good. What the market needs is fresh cash to move it up. Money speaks louder than words. If the market starts to stumble though, these stockholders may start bailing out, thus depressing prices even more. No, the bulls can't help that market by themselves, and they have the potential to hurt it. The bears, though, are a potential reservoir of new money. When the newsletter writers are extremely bearish, their subscribers are usually in cash. That's a setup for a market rebound when that cash returns to the market.

Now, I'm referring to extremes of newsletter sentiment. If over 65 percent of those advisers are bullish and have stabilized near that level, look for a market correction—perhaps a severe one. If over 50 percent are bearish and have been there for a few weeks, start preparing your shopping list.

What if newsletter sentiment is not at those extremes but has been changing rapidly? Then go with the trend. As the advisers are changing from bearish to bullish, cash is pouring into the market. That is indeed bullish. Stay with the crowd until sentiment becomes extreme. The converse is true, of course. As the writers are steadily switching from bullish to bearish, money will be withdrawn from the market and prices will decline until the sentiment stabilizes.

Another important indicator, with shorter-term implications, is the *put/call ratio*. This most specifically refers to listed stock options traded on the Chicago Board Options Exchange, a place I used to report from every market day. This is not the place to go into an entire treatise on options. But, simply stated, the purchaser of a *call option* is making a leveraged bet that a certain stock or index will move up significantly in the near future. Conversely, the purchaser of a *put option* is looking for the stock to decline. Of course, the sellers of put and call options hope for the opposite, but they are often the designated traders on the exchange floor who must make a market in certain options. Most of those professional traders make a really nice steady income selling the options. Nonprofessionals who sell (or write) covered options also tend to come out ahead in the long run. It's those short-term speculators who run with their emotions (remember fear and greed), who buy the options and tend to be on the wrong side. More calls are normally purchased than puts. If the ratio of puts sold during a day becomes more than 75 percent of the calls, bearish sentiment is becoming extreme. This usually occurs near the end of a market decline. It's a sign that the market is about to rebound from an oversold condition. Conversely, if the put/call ratio falls under 50 percent, bullish speculation is running rampant and a setback may be in sight.

Also related to options is the *volatility index* or VIX. Strictly speaking, this is not actually a measure of recent price volatility, but instead it is an indicator of how much market participants believe prices will fluctuate in the near future. The VIX is calculated by running current option premiums through a complex standard model. When the VIX gets into the 40 to 50 range, fear is running rampant. Prices have undoubtedly been declining for a while, and some people are worrying about a final crash. More likely, it points to a buying opportunity for those who still have their heads on straight.

CLEVER INVENTIONS

The *Arms Index* or TRIN (Trading Index) was invented in the 1960s by New Mexico–based money manager Richard Arms. The Web site is *www.armsinsider.com*. It's a little complicated because it involves three ratios. The first ratio is the number of advancing issues on the New York Stock Exchange during one day divided by the declining issues. The share volume represented by those advancing issues is then divided by the declining volume to get a second ratio. Finally, the first ratio is divided by the second ratio to get the Arms Index. A ratio of 1.0 is neutral. Readings above 1.0 indicate short-term bearishness and readings below 1.0 indicate short-term bullishness. I know that seems counterintuitive, and so does Richard Arms. He once told me that he wished he had inverted the ratio so that higher numbers indicated bullishness, but the index became popular quickly and couldn't be changed. Thus, this model is best interpreted in a contrary manner. If the day ends with a high Arms Index over 2.5, the bears have been running rampant and a rally may soon follow. And if you see readings around 0.4, get ready for a market correction. We will be discussing the Arms Index in more depth in a later chapter. (Richard Arms has written the books *The Arms Index* and *Profits in Volume*. They and others are available on his Web site.)

An even more complex model is the McClellan Oscillator invented by Sherman McClellan and his wife Marian over 30 years ago. It is a terrific improvement on the old advance/decline ratio. McClellan and his son Tom still use it as an integral part of the *McClellan Market Report*. It's a fine tool that I use myself and will cover in more detail in a later chapter. You can get a description by going to the Web site *www.mcoscillator.com* and clicking Oscillator. I suggest you check it out.

THE GOLDEN RATIO

A simple but important ratio is the *golden ratio* of the ancient Greeks. It's often given as 0.618 or about 62 percent. With more precision, it's 0.61803398875. It can be found easily on your calculator by taking the square root of 1.25 and subtracting 0.5. It's sometimes called the *Fibonacci ratio* after a medieval mathematician. Here we'll simply call it G. Take out your calculator and try dividing 1 by G. Surprised? It's 1.61803398875—exactly 1 more than G. In fact, this inverted result is also often given as the golden ratio; we'll call it $G1$. Now square G. You get 0.3819660113. We'll call that $G2$. Then add G to $G2$. Voilà, it's 1. Now square $G1$. How about that? The result is exactly 1 greater than $G1$.

The golden ratio is often seen in nature, as with the growth of a helical seashell. It's regularly demonstrated in art and architecture as a pleasing proportion for framing a picture or designing a building. In the marketplace, G or its derivatives frequently limit the extent of a trend. It's not unusual for a stock price to give back 38 percent ($G2$) or 62 percent (G) of a recent run-up. Conversely, it will often rally 38 or 62 percent of a recent decline. The more that you follow the market technically, the more you will be amazed how these percentages crop up. You may want to add knowledge of the golden ratio to your technical tool kit. It may alert you that a trend is about to reverse, just when everyone else believes there is no end in sight.

ACTIVITY CREATES MOVEMENT
Why Volume Counts

When a stock is thinly traded, it can stay in a well-defined price channel for a long time. Those who follow the company know that they can find buyers at the lower portion of that channel and sellers up near the top. As long as there is no news of significance, it seems to stay in that range endlessly. But then one day, with the stock in the high end of its range, the trading volume picks up quite noticeably. The price may move up only slightly as fresh demand rakes in the stock of the willing sellers at that level. Once all those sellers have gotten out at their price, the stock price then spurts upward. Now it grabs the attention of others who sense that something must be happening with the company, and they clamor on board. Trading volume accelerates as does the price. The stock is taking off in a new bull run.

A few weeks later, the company announces better than expected earnings. It also lets us know that a new breakthrough product is under development that could contribute hugely to earnings in the future. The stock spurts upward the morning of the announcement, then pulls back and actually closes down at the end of the day. That is known as "selling on the news," a form of "profit taking." More sophisticated investors had already anticipated the news and were only too glad to cash in by selling to late comers who had been reluctant to get in before the solid news was in hand. The new buyers would have expected the news to propel the stock even further. It did—immediately before they bought.

Possibly the eventual good news had been rumored, possibly not. But technically oriented investors could have inferred that something was happening with the company, and that it was probably beneficial. They saw this with the initial increase in trading volume followed by a rising price. It told them that somebody must know something. It was not necessarily company insiders who were buying initially; although it could have been. It may have been low-level employees who were leaking information to friends and relatives. Suppliers or customers of the company might have surmised that business had been picking up or new products were under development.

These inferences would not likely have reached the financial news media, but technically oriented investors noticed the increase in trading volume followed by price movement. This alerted them to get into the stock, despite any solid evidence of good news. Once the news was announced and everyone was aware of it, thus fully pricing it into the market, the traders bailed out. They had no further reason to be in and needed the money for the next opportunity they had detected.

Money talks. Although information may be kept under some degree of control, those who know or sense something reveal themselves by their actions in the marketplace. They may not be moving their mouths, but what they do with their money speaks volumes.

MARKET VOLUME

There will be periods in the market during which emotions are running high. The trading volume may be unusually great for not just one stock, but the entire market. An October Monday in 1987 marked the climax of one of those periods. The bull had been charging for 5 years. The Dow was under 800 in August of 1982 and rose above 2700 in August of 1987. Then stock prices began easing. Particularly in 1986 and earlier in 1987, traders had learned to buy on dips. But now rallies following dips had little force or duration. More people than ever before were investing in stocks. And they began to get scared. Typical daily trading volume in New York had risen from under 100 million to over 200 million. After several 100-point down days on the Dow, investors were really fretting. Friday, October 16, an options expiration day, was one of those days. Talk of a crash was in the air. And it came.

On Monday, October 19, the bottom fell out. The Dow fell 22 percent from above 2200 to nearly 1700. NYSE volume surged to above 600 million shares. Everyone was running for the exit at the same time. The next morning, more tried to get out as talk of economic disaster filled the air. Folks remembered how the Crash of 1929 resulted in the Great Depression and, eventually, much lower stock prices. But cooler heads saw no signs of economic problems and properly assessed that they had just witnessed a panic that presented them with an opportunity. They bought—and bought heavily. A significant portion of the previous day's losses were recouped. And the trading volume was just as high. This V-shaped pattern of price along with unprecedented volume told the alert technician that he or she had witnessed a washout producing a greatly oversold market. Since "Black Monday," the Dow has never closed lower. And there was no recession for another 3 years. Those with cool heads and eyes on price and volume profited handsomely.

When we get to the chapters in which we study specific technical patterns, we will see many examples of how volume reinforces our interpretation of the price movement. Price and volume work together like hand and glove. Always try to be aware of both.

Technical Analysis

4

NOT SO FUNDAMENTAL

Why the Value Game Lets You Down

While in business college, I took a number of courses in accounting and finance; all business students do. In accounting classes, we learned how to determine the so-called book value of a company. In finance classes, we learned more sophisticated methods for valuing a company. Many of these models involve the ratios presented in Chapter 3. But once one has determined all of these measures of a firm's financial health, how does one assign a fair stock price? Those who attempt to determine value through these "fundamental" methods can only go by the historical norm. They must take into account the prevailing level of interest rates to get an idea of how much investors are currently expecting as a rate of return on their money. Then they value the stock at a level commensurate with companies that exhibited similar statistics in the past while interest rates were comparable to the current ones.

The price-earnings ratio (P/E) is probably the most relied upon measure in making these determinations. The price, of course, is fact. The earnings, as we learned early in the twenty-first century, cannot always be precisely determined or even relied upon. Nevertheless, the P/E for an individual stock, an industry, or the entire market does tend to move inversely to interest rates. But the correlation is not precise. Investor sentiment plays a big factor. That sentiment may be based purely on emotions or on more substantial evidence regarding future prospects.

In the late nineties, P/E ratios got way out of line, at least when compared with sound fundamental analysis. When this occurs, it's usually a setup for a crash. But that crash can be a long time in coming. The market by traditional standards was hugely overvalued in October 1999. But if you had "wisely" exited the market at that time, you would have missed the Nasdaq composite doubling over the next 5 months. The smart move would have been to have persevered until March 2000. The fundamentals would not have told you precisely when the bell would be ringing. Even solid technical work would not have told you that Friday, March 10, would be the day, although good cycle analysis could have given a clue. But not long after the peak, the technical charts began to hint that the party had ended and it might be wise to step aside and let others ride the market down.

Back in the summer of 1982, interest rates were astronomical, as was the rate of inflation. Earnings were poor. The fundamentalists told us that stock prices should be quite low. And indeed they were. All the advice was to put your money in those newfangled, high-yielding money market funds. And people did just that. So most investors were caught flat-footed on Friday the thirteenth (so much for that superstition) of August, when the market launched into the most fabulous bull market ever witnessed. And it lasted for 17½ years. Technical analysis may not have put you into the market on the twelfth of August, but it would have gotten you in shortly thereafter. And it would have kept you in during most of the rest of the eighties and the nineties.

5

THE MARKET'S MIND

You Can Read It in the Charts

Some anthropologists say that our ancestors first became truly human about 50,000 years ago when they learned how to read minds. No, I don't mean that in the psychic sense. I'm referring to the ability to infer what other people know, think, or feel. Most of us begin demonstrating this ability when we're about 4 years old. That's why traditional kindergartens limit their enrollment to 5-year-olds. Adult apes are no better than human 3-year-olds in this faculty. Elementary schools want little people who have attained some degree of social skill.

This type of mind reading can make insider trading a really gray area. A corporate officer may try her best not to reveal insider information to her friends. Sometimes it is what is *not* said or topics that are avoided that give others a clue to what might be happening. Then, if a friend acts on his intuition, sells the stock, and it plummets the next day because of a piece of bad news, prosecutors move in. And often the circumstantial evidence is compelling enough to get a conviction, much to the chagrin of the insider and her friend, who are still convinced of their innocence.

Until the twentieth century, savvy traders intuitively sensed what might be happening within a company based on the price and volume activity of its stock. In earlier times, this was purely an art since very little of the science attached to this had been developed.

But even then, traders would clamber on board a stock when its price and volume picked up. And they would do this for no other reason than the sense that some folks must know something or they would not be trading their hard-earned dollars for stock shares. Often, however, the moves turned out to be false and the trades turned into losers.

Eventually, more diligent researchers were able to discern which trading patterns were more likely to be predictive of future price action. Even the extent of the current move could be estimated with some degree of confidence.

Trading ranges became recognized with well-defined support and resistance levels. At the lower end of the range, willing buyers could be counted on to appear as they sensed a bargain. At the upper end, willing sellers were assembled and ready to take profits. A technically alert trader did not actually have to be aware of the existence of these people. He or she could infer their presence by the trading pattern in the stock chart. And, of course, could take advantage of this insight by timing his or her own trades appropriately.

Breakouts from trading ranges accompanied by volume spikes became recognized as the advent of moves to new price territory. Alert technicians did not need to know why the breakout was occurring. They just recognized that some unknown factor was kindling interest and that they would be well advised to take action themselves.

Over time, a whole array of reliable trading patterns became the foundation of technical analysis. These patterns will be the subject of much of the rest of this book.

6

BASIC ANATOMY

The ABCs of Charting

Now we come to what we've been building toward, the basics of technical analysis. Folks may have told you that technical analysis is all voodoo mumbo jumbo. No, it's not astrology or rune casting. The earlier chapters of this book were designed to give you an understanding of why technical analysis works. We market technicians study what people are actually doing with their money. We pore over the price and volume charts to find patterns suggestive of future price direction. We may not know why the buyers and sellers are doing what they are doing. The underlying motivations may not become evident until well after a price move occurs. But if you wait to make your move until after the news comes out, you will have missed an opportunity to profit. Yes, it's always easier to justify a decision when all of the facts are in hand. Unfortunately, in the marketplace you have to be there ahead of the crowd in order to do well. And that involves taking some chances with educated assessments based on technical analysis. You won't always be right, but in the long run you should end up well ahead of those who are not able to read the messages sent by the charts.

I used the word *charts*. Perhaps a more common term is *graphs*, and that is what a statistician or mathematician would call them. *Chart* is actually a more generic term applying to varying types of visual representations. But we market technicians have long referred to our graphs as charts, and we will continue that convention here.

THE BAR

Let's examine the essentials of a technical chart. Figure 6-1 was designed to help us do that. As with most graphs in which time is a variable, time is illustrated on the horizontal axis. The earliest time is to the left, the latest to the right. Our model chart represents one market week of trading with Monday on the left and Friday on the right. Price is represented on the upper portion of the vertical axis. The lowest price is near the bottom; the highest is near the top. The volume of shares traded in each time period (usually a day in this book) is seen in the lower portion of the vertical axis. The greater the trading volume, the higher the volume bar rises. As with most examples in this book, the actual dates, prices, and volume levels are not shown. This is done to reduce clutter. Only the relative values need be known in order to grasp the concepts. Most of the concepts apply both to short-term and long-term charts. A long-term investor may study charts that are several years in length with each bar representing a week's trading. A day trader may study the chart of a single day with each bar representing 5 minutes of activity. Yet both charts may look similar, and the same principles can apply.

Let's examine an individual price bar more carefully. Note in Figure 6-1 how the Wednesday (middle) bar is labeled. The vertical extent of the bar depicts the day's price range. The top of the bar represents the day's high price, and the bottom shows the low price. The tick mark to the left points to the price at which the stock first traded (opening) that day. The tick mark to the right indicates the level of the final trade (closing) of the day. Most of the charts in this book will depict trading bars in this form. A similar form will be seen in other sources, although frequently the opening price may be omitted.

THE CHART

Let's take a look at a simple chart that we will encounter again later when it's discussed in more detail. As with the majority of our charts, it depicts a simplified trading world in order to make the key concepts stand out. Figure 6-2 shows trading in a stock over a period of 13 weeks, 65 trading days. Within a general price uptrend, we note that the price moves into a trading range for about 7 weeks

FIGURE 6-1

Model Bars

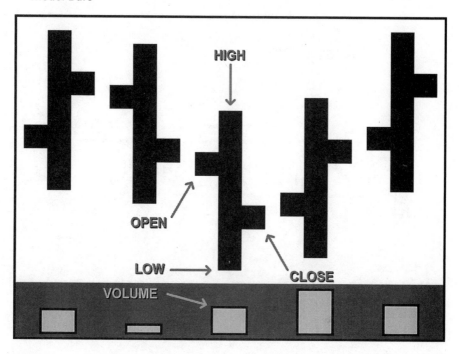

in the middle of the chart. This range is defined by two price levels: the support level and the resistance level. The *support level* is the price that buyers repeatedly find to be attractive. They step in and buy here, thus stemming any further decline. The *resistance level* is the price at which sellers can't resist accepting profits. Here they repeatedly sell, thus halting any further rise. Eventually, one of these two camps becomes exhausted, and the stock price breaks through to new territory. In the illustrated case, the stock breaks out to the upside, since those who had been willing to sell at the resistance level are no longer offering shares. Perhaps they have no more. That could be because of aggressive buyers who suddenly bought out the supply at that level. However, it could also be that the sellers suddenly saw greater value in the stock and retracted their offers. In any event, it's off to the races for a while. Note that volume slowed while the price entered a trading range. Then volume spiked upward as the stock broke out of the trading range. That would have been

FIGURE 6-2

Model Chart

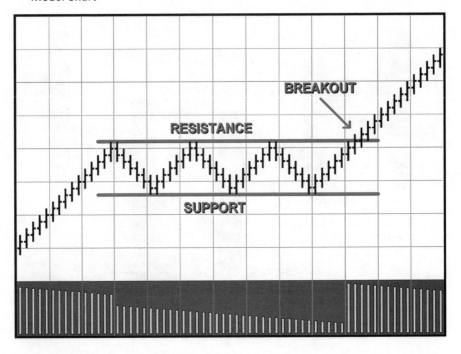

strong confirmation that the breakout was for real and the upward move may continue for a while.

The basic format seen in Figure 6-2 will be repeated in many of the charts included in this book. However, the specific patterns and their implications for the future will vary quite a bit. For most of the book, the support and resistance lines will be provided and will point to critical junctures. Toward the end of the book, you will be presented with charts in which you will have to draw in the barrier lines and infer the future price movement. You may surprise yourself when you find how easily you will be able to do this.

After you have mastered the tests, you will want to apply what you have learned to real-world charts. I wouldn't advise actually backing up your predictions with serious money until you have proven to yourself that you have become an adept market technician. The more you practice, the better you will probably become. Eventually, there is a good chance that you will amaze yourself when your predictions come true. Then just when you start expecting to be right every time, some bizarre event will slap you in the face and produce a loss. You'll never win them all. But you should learn from your mistakes. Maybe the event was not really so bizarre and could have been anticipated if the chart had been analyzed correctly.

Although most charts in this book have been standardized to cover an intermediate-term period of 13 weeks, the principles illustrated can be applied to shorter and longer terms. An in-and-out day trader may look at a similar chart of only an hour's duration, with each bar representing a minute of trading. A long-term investor may examine a chart that covers 5 or 10 years, with each bar depicting a month of trading. As with fractal geometry (a principle to be discussed in greater detail in Chapter 12 on Elliott wave analysis) similar patterns will often be seen in compressed or expanded time frames.

Eventually the identification of these standard patterns will become second nature to you, and you will be able to intuitively sense the direction of the next price move. So take the time to let all of the patterns sink into your consciousness. The basic patterns in the next chapters will cover more than 90 percent of the situations that you will encounter. Yes, there are many more patterns that have been noted by technicians. But I wouldn't advise moving to the more advanced texts that cover them in detail until you have fully internalized the basics. So let us proceed.

7

UPTRENDING PATTERNS

The Trend Is Your Friend

We'll begin our survey of common technical patterns with the easy case. That would be an uptrending market, the kind that most folks wish were the only case. Actually, it is the most common case, with the market and individual stocks uptrending the majority of the time. Bull markets normally have at least twice the duration of the intervening bear markets.

Uptrends begin when a few knowledgeable investors see value in depressed prices. Perhaps they have reason to believe that business conditions will improve for a specific company or the economy in general. Others may simply be lucky speculators. Lucky this time, that is. They may have unwisely been buying on dips all the way down. Now they finally seem to be getting it right and can brag about it. Once the trend gets moving, a few others will get on board, figuring that those earlier buyers must know something. Later, we actually start to hear news that business is getting a bit better. More buy in upon hearing this. As the news continues to improve, even more investors become confident and start buying. Eventually, after the news is all good and the market has moved up impressively, the most cautious investors finally cash in their bonds and buy stocks. They needed that much proof that we were actually in a bull market. The key word was *were*, as this is the point at which the bubble normally bursts. We saw this most dramatically in late 1999 and early 2000. The uptrend ends and a new bear market begins because all potential buyers are already in the market. Their cheering will do no good. Fresh money is needed to move the market further, and that has all been used up. Now there are a lot of people whose only options are to hold or sell. And selling, of course, will depress prices. Those last buyers are often referred to as the "greater fools." This refers to the answer given by a buyer who is accused of being a fool for buying into a speculative bull market. That person will say that a greater fool is sure to come along to take his or her stocks away at a higher price.

We're now going to examine the period in which the market or a stock is past the bottoming process but is not approaching its peak. This is termed the happy phase, the uptrending phase, the heart of a bull market.

Uptrends, of course, are not continuous. The market or an individual stock certainly will not move up each and every day over an extended period of time, regardless of how strong the trend is. But over a period of weeks, there is often a tendency for stocks to keep rising at a sustained pace, even though the daily movement may show zigs and zags. Figure 7-1 is an idealized example of this pattern. We see an up and down pattern repeating about every 12 trading days within the context of a major uptrend. Each time the stock goes through its cycle, the buyers step in at somewhat higher prices than the previous lows. The sellers hold out for more at each new high. These tendencies allow the market technician to detect a trading channel with upward-sloping support and resistance levels. The support level is the price area in which buyers tend to come into the market. The resistance level is that zone in which sellers take their profits.

The market technician takes out his or her straightedge and connects the bottoms of all the dips. The *support line* has now been drawn. The same is done with each of the peaks. That gives the *resistance line*. The technician will assume that the stock price will continue to trace a path within this channel. Of course, it will eventually break out one way or the other. Notice how the volume peaks in the midst of each minirally and troughs in the midst of each minicorrection. That is strong evidence that the market remains in a solidly bullish phase.

Figure 7-2 is a more true-to-life example of the impulse phase of a bull market. Don't always expect the support and resistance

FIGURE 7-1

Ideal Uptrend

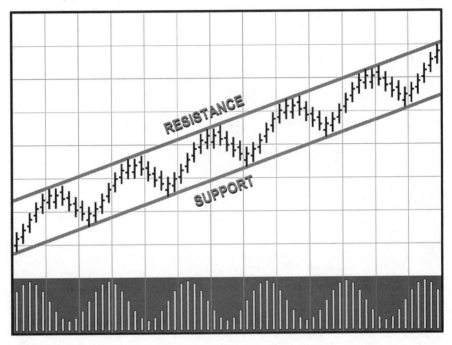

levels to fit reality with perfect neatness. With more experience, you will be able to judge when a pattern is just a variant of the archetype and when it may be something else entirely.

If the price breaks out of the channel to the upside, that may imply a powerful but final burst of enthusiasm before a truly significant correction. Such a thing happened most dramatically for a broad range of companies in late 1999. The Nasdaq Composite doubled from October 1999 to March 2000. We all know what happened after that: no mere correction but a protracted bear market. However, if this were to occur after the market had recently completed a bottoming formation and begun a rise, it may signal an extended period of even swifter price increases.

If the price breaks beneath the downside of the channel, the implication is that the solid rally phase is over and the market is due for at least a rest. It may mean even worse than that. To be more confident in our prediction, we'll have to look at more evidence than we'll find in Figures 7-1 or 7-2.

FIGURE 7-2

Realistic Uptrend

BULLISH FLAG FORMATIONS

We saw Figure 7-3 earlier, when we were learning the basic geometry of a chart from Figure 6-2. Indeed, it is highly simplified. Most
of the charts in this book have the clutter removed so that we can
attune our eyes to the basic patterns. Figure 7-3 idealizes a *bullish flag
formation*. The pole of the flag is seen in the early price bars to the
left. Here we see a nice steady uptrend, the kind that everyone
wishes could be unending. Then the stock enters a price range as its
price zigzags within a channel. And this is a well-defined channel
with easy to see support and resistance areas. In this case the stock
stays in this channel for about 7 weeks. It reminds one of a flag as
it waves up and down. Do the support and resistance lines have to
be perfectly horizontal? No, they can slightly uptrend or downtrend. But the two lines should be nearly parallel to be called a *flag
formation*. In the case of a bullish flag formation, the flag more often
droops a bit, giving us down-sloping support and resistance lines.

FIGURE 7-3

Ideal Bullish Flag

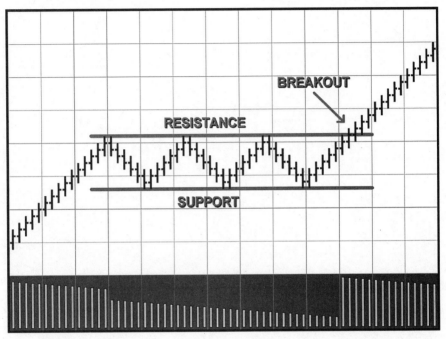

We see this in Figure 7-4, which also gives us a more realistic pattern of trading.

The expectation is that the price will eventually break out of its trading range in the same direction in which it entered. That is up. It may not. But if it does, we expect a rally with an extent similar to the one seen before the entrance into the channel. Do notice here how the volume in Figure 7-3, which had been drifting lower during the trading range, suddenly spikes upward as the price breaks out above that range. That is strong confirmation that the breakout is for real and significant price appreciation can be expected in the near future. In the case of Figure 7-4, we see the price hesitating for several days at the resistance level on high volume before the sellers are cleared out of the way. Then the price is free to move up dramatically, continuing the uptrend that we saw before entering the trading channel.

Flag formations are quite common in a bull market. They give the market a chance to digest earlier gains without significant giveback.

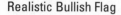

FIGURE 7-4

Realistic Bullish Flag

You may observe a number of bullish flags over a period of months, or even years. They are a healthy sign that the bull market is still intact and has not yet entered the final speculative phase.

BULLISH PENNANT FORMATIONS

Closely related to the bullish flag formation is the *bullish pennant formation* as idealized in Figure 7-5. Here we enter the pattern in a fashion similar to the flag. However, while the flag was confined by nearly parallel support and resistance lines, the pennant is a bit different. In the case of bullish pennant formation, the support line is nearly horizontal while the resistance line tends to slope downward. This implies that buyers continuously find the stock priced attractively at a certain level. But the sellers become more aggressive each time the stock price makes a modest rally. Eventually, the two groups meet at the point of the pennant. One

FIGURE 7-5

Ideal Bullish Pennant

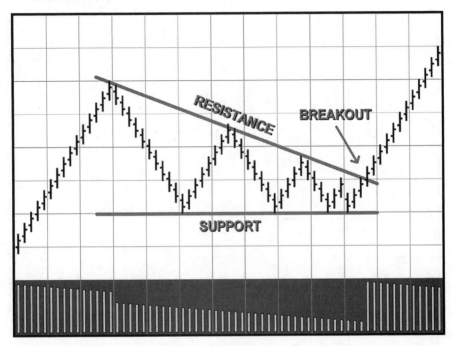

of the two groups will be more powerful than the other. The weaker group will have all of its orders filled, leaving the stronger to keep pushing the market in its direction. If the buyers prevail, then we have a true bullish pennant formation. Volume should spike upward and the rally should be seen before entering the trading range then resumes.

Figure 7-6 shows a more realistic version of a bullish pennant formation. In this case, the support line is not precisely horizontal. Also, the support line is slightly penetrated on an intraday basis, but never on a closing basis. It would certainly make life easier for a market technician if charts looked more like Figure 7-5, but in the real world you'll have to accept the imperfections of charts like Figure 7-6. It will take experience to know when to allow for imperfections while still accepting that the basic pattern applies. This ability will come, and the entire process will seem more intuitive with time. We'll be discussing how this process evolves in Chapter 14.

FIGURE 7-6

Realistic Bullish Pennant

BULLISH WEDGE FORMATION

A *bullish wedge formation* is slightly different from a bullish pennant formation. Some would argue that the pennant is a type of wedge, but there are some differences. Figure 7-7 shows an idealized bullish wedge formation. It begins when a strong uptrend runs into resistance and enters a trading range. We've seen this in some of the earlier patterns. Notice how the support level slopes upward within the trading range and the resistance level slopes downward. The two eventually converge at a point of confrontation between large groups of buyers and sellers. Notice how the volume, which had already started to taper off, gets even softer while in the trading range. At the point of convergence, the bulls and bears do battle. If the bulls are the larger group, which is the expected case as this type of pattern unfolds, they buy up all of the offered shares at the level of convergence and cause the price to break out to the upside.

FIGURE 7-7

Ideal Bullish Wedge

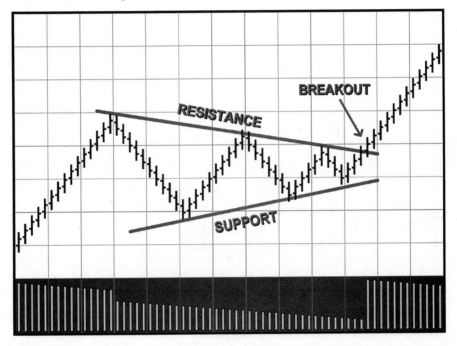

Volume should spurt upward during this process. This is a resumption of the original bullish trend as the volume rises to stronger levels.

Figure 7-8 is a more realistic example of a bullish wedge formation. It's not quite as neat as Figure 7-7, but the real world never is. Nevertheless, it clearly demonstrates the basic pattern of a bullish wedge. Notice how it shows a bit of hesitation at the breakout, as the last of the aggressive sellers are cleared out of the way. This is a common occurrence and frustrating for those who expect confirmation to come during a single trading day. It's not often that easy, and patience becomes a virtue. Reacting to single-day moves can result in a trader getting "whipsawed." This occurs when the trader anticipates a signal with scant evidence and then is forced to reverse his or her position when more solid information emerges.

FIGURE 7-8

Realistic Bullish Wedge

UPTREND SUMMARY

An uptrending market is the happy time. It is also the usual case. It will rarely run unhesitatingly upward. External news and investor psychology will present us with periodic corrections. These are healthy and prevent the market from frequently entering a bubble phase. Bubbles burst and lead to long-term bear markets. But by studying archetypal bullish flag formations, bullish pennant formations, and bullish wedge formations, we learn how to recognize the points at which the market is merely getting back its breath during a greater bull trend. Next we'll look at the frustrating part of market watching, a downtrending market.

8

DOWNTRENDING PATTERNS

Endless Pressure

In Chapter 7, we examined continuation patterns in a bull market. That was the fun part. Long-term investors could buy and hold. Short-term traders would usually do well, so long as they avoided going short too often. Now we look at the opposite situation. Bear markets can be frustrating, not to mention destructive of your wealth. Folks are often advised to buy and hold, being told that they can't go wrong in the long run. Sometimes these advisers say that because they don't want to be accused of "churning"(that is, instigating a client to trade frequently in order to generate continuous commissions). Such concern is genuine, since a broker could lose his or her registration if convicted of such a tactic. Unfortunately, the long run for which people are asked to buy and hold can be a very long time indeed.

Most people who bought at the 1929 peak had to wait nearly 30 years to get even. And by then, the value of the dollar had substantially eroded. Those who bought in 1966 didn't see any progress until the market took off in the summer of 1982. Those who bought in 1999 or 2000 are still waiting to get even as this book is being written. Even the few years since then have been an immensely frustrating period for those who had such high hopes that a "new" economy would ensure an early and comfortable retirement. Many just kept riding the market down in the hope that the good old days would soon return.

How can we avoid such stubbornness? By reading the charts. In this chapter we'll examine some of the basic models that warn us that a bear market will linger for a while. The signals we glean may tell us to get out at a loss. But we must learn to accept small losses before they turn into something catastrophic. Too many people take profits too early in a bull market and concede their losses too late in a bear market. We all want to claim we're winners, no matter how small the prize. No one wants to admit to being a loser, even if the loss is quite modest. If you want to be a successful investor, you have to get out of this rut. Do what the charts are telling you to do. Run with the winners and abandon the losers.

Figure 8-1 demonstrates the basic model for a downtrend, a bear market. The support and resistance lines continuously slope downward. The sellers become more aggressive as time advances,

FIGURE 8-1

Ideal Downtrend

and the buyers become more reluctant. The market does not move down every day, but the down-moves outweigh the up-moves. In this idealized example, the market remains within the channel bounded by the support and resistance lines. Notice how the volume peaks when the price is moving down most rapidly, and troughs when prices are temporarily rising. It reminds us of many periods in the market during the early 2000s. Investors just kept riding the market down out of pure hope, when there were no indications that the situation would turn around. We'll get to those reversal patterns in Chapters 9 and 10. But here we'll look for signs that the overall downtrend is still intact.

Figure 8-2 gives us a more realistic view of a nevertheless relentless downtrend. The support and resistance lines are not always met exactly, but the price tracing comes close. So long as the support and resistance lines contain the market, the trend is expected to remain intact. Any meaningful reversal may still be a long way off.

FIGURE 8-2

Realistic Downtrend

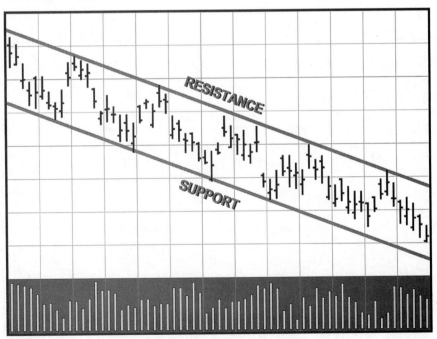

BEARISH FLAG FORMATIONS

Figure 8-3 shows us the basic pattern for a *bearish flag formation*. Here we see what had been an uninterrupted downtrend entering a trading channel. We see something like an upside-down flagpole and then a waving flag. The market then meanders between parallel support and resistance levels for a number of weeks. In the idealized example, the support and resistance lines run horizontally. They could slope slightly upward, which is a common case. Or they could slope downward. The important thing is that the two lines are roughly parallel with a true flag formation. When we see the price breakdown below the trading support level on heavy volume, we have a sign that the bear trend remains intact and is about to move rapidly again to lower levels. Notice how the volume slowed down while the market was in the trading range and spurted upward when the price broke below.

Figure 8-4 demonstrates a more realistic bearish flag formation. In this example, the price begins to penetrate the support level for

FIGURE 8-3

Ideal Bearish Flag

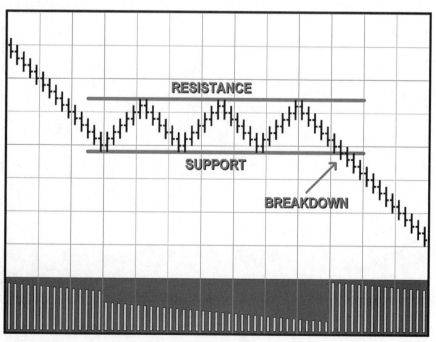

FIGURE 8-4

Realistic Bearish Flag

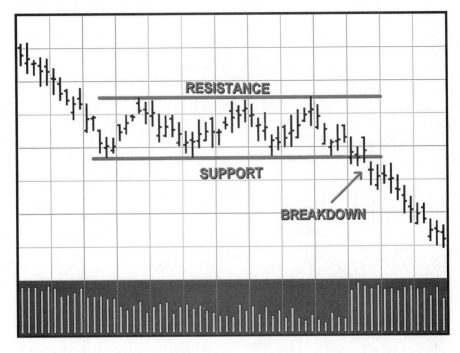

a few days on an intraday basis only. That's a common signal that bad things are about to happen. Here, when the price does move through support on a closing basis, it does so cleanly. And it does so on heavy volume. When you see this, stay on the sidelines. The bear is about to go on another rampage. The market is telling you that this is what will happen by the price action and its accompanying volume. It doesn't care what you are hoping it will do. Hopes don't matter in the marketplace. The market doesn't care what you want. It only responds positively if you and a lot of other people feed it money.

BEARISH PENNANT FORMATIONS

Figure 8-5 is an archetypal model for a *bearish pennant formation*. This is closely related to a bearish flag formation, but with a tapering flag that resembles a pennant. We see a strong downtrend that seems to reverse as it enters the pennant. We now see an uptrending support

FIGURE 8-5

Ideal Bearish Pennant

line that gives many investors cause for hope that the bear market has ended. The clue that it has not ended comes when the second leg up goes no higher than the first. Despite the upward-sloping support line, we see a horizontal resistance line that seems to be stiff resistance indeed. Eventually the two lines converge. At the point of convergence, the two camps battle it out. We should not be surprised if the bulls are still outnumbered and are forced to retreat. When the price breaks down beneath the support line on heavy volume, head for the hills as prices are likely to cascade downward even more.

Figure 8-6 is a more real-world example of a bearish pennant formation. The support and resistance lines are not quite so neat and clear-cut as in Figure 8-5, but the pattern should still be recognizable. When the price moves out of the pennant shaped trading channel on heavy volume, the meaning is still unmistakable. The overall trend is still down, and one should not expect a significant reversal to the upside for some time to come.

FIGURE 8-6

Realistic Bearish Pennant

These bearish continuation patterns are indeed frustrating. But one should try not to deny their existence. Recognizing that a bearish trend is still intact is important for the preservation of your wealth.

BEARISH WEDGE FORMATIONS

Figure 8-7 shows us a clean example of a *bearish wedge formation*. Again we see a downtrending market enter into a trading range. Unlike the pennant, we see a definitely downtrending resistance line. This has even more bearish implications than the pennant, because the sellers become more aggressive as the pattern unfolds. As the wedge converges to a point, the buyers and sellers meet to do battle. As expected, the sellers overwhelm the buyers. As the potential buyers are cleared out, the price breaks beneath the support level on increased volume. That's a clear sign that hope should be abandoned for now.

F I G U R E 8-7

Ideal Bearish Wedge

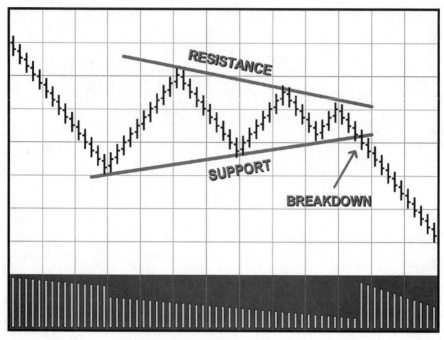

Figure 8-8 gives us a more realistic view of a bearish wedge formation. The support and resistance lines cannot be drawn so neatly as in the previous example. But the wedge pattern should be jumping out at you. Notice how, after the first clean break beneath the support line, a brief attempt was made to rally back. But that little rally fizzled quickly. Such an occurrence gives us further confirmation of the breakdown. Expect much lower prices before a good long-term buying opportunity arises.

DOWNTREND SUMMARY

A bear market for an individual stock or the overall market can be relentless. Yes, the patterns that you see in this book apply to both single companies and the market as a whole. Buy-and-hold investors are frustrated, but tend to hold on to their positions. Early in the

FIGURE 8-8

Realistic Bearish Wedge

bear market, these investors believe they are witnessing just a little bit of the usual profit taking. Later on, they are sure that the strong headwind will eventually turn around and profits will soon be reemerging. Finally, they start to feel exhausted and only hang on in the hope of getting back their original investments. The wait could be a long time indeed.

When you recognize that a bear trend is in force, stop counting on hope to extend your profits or minimize your losses. Take your profits, if you still have them. Accept your losses while they are still modest. That will leave you with a stash of cash to put to work when the next bull market is in swing. Doing what the charts tell you, and not what your heart is saying, is right and will leave you a much wealthier person.

In Chapters 6 and 7 we examined continuation patterns. These are the charts that tell us that the trend of the market is likely to endure for quite a while, despite occasional journeys in the opposite direction. Most of the time, a stock or the market is likely to continue its trend. That trend will usually end only when all the buyers or sellers are used up. Then certain developments begin to be sensed. Either the microeconomy of an individual company or the greater macroeconomy is about to turn. This is often first signaled in the reversal patterns that we will study in Chapters 9 and 10. Don't count on the reasons behind the reversal to appear in the news for some time.

9

TOPPING FORMATIONS

Time to Step Away from the Crowd

Until now, we have been looking at continuation patterns, those charts that indicate that the primary trend of the market is still intact. Now we begin our look at reversal patterns, charts that give us a clue that the tide has turned.

In Chapter 7 we examined the uptrending patterns prevalent during a bull market. In Chapter 8 we observed the downtrending patterns that prevail during a bear market. In this chapter and Chapter 10, we will look at those formations that tell us when we have shifted from one trend to the other.

First, we will look at topping formations. When we were examining bull trends in Chapter 7, we saw that the trend was sometimes interrupted and the price of a stock or the overall market moved into a trading range. We saw examples in which the trading range was merely a pause for the market to regain its breath before the uptrend resumed. More often than not, that bull trend does resume. Eventually, though, the bull gets long in the tooth. As the bull market approaches its ultimate conclusion, investors are at their most optimistic.

It's only natural that prices will be at their highest when the greatest number of people are expectant of even higher prices. The thing that makes a stock desirable, of course, is the belief that its price will rise. So the price hits its peak when the greatest number of believers are already shareholders. Once everybody is onboard, all they can do is cheer. As we've noted before, cheering cannot move the market. Only fresh cash can drive it upward.

We eventually reach a point at which current shareholders start taking profits in larger numbers. At the same time, fewer new buyers are out there. The bear starts growling as sellers are forced to accept lower prices if they want to find buyers.

This hesitancy for prices to make further upward progress can be gleaned from the charts. If we look carefully, we can detect points at which the buying interest is no longer sufficient to match the selling pressure. The transition rarely comes in the form of an inverted V. There is usually some vacillation at the turning point. But a few basic patterns tend to appear again and again at market turns. They give us strong clues that the bull market may have ended.

HEAD AND SHOULDERS FORMATION

First, we will take a look at one of the most famous technical patterns. It is also my personal favorite. The *head and shoulders formation* seems to be the one that almost all investors have at least heard about. Is it a good one? No, not if you're a stubborn bull. But it can be a very good friend that warns you of impending doom if you happen to be listening. Figure 9-1 shows us the ideal head and shoulders formation. The price pattern traces the outline of a person's head surrounded by two prominent shoulders. The human mind is wired to imagine human or animal shapes in inanimate objects ranging from clouds to mountains on Mars. It's no different when we see functions traced on a graph.

In Figure 9-1, we see on the left a bull market that is still uptrending. But volume is low relative to what it had been. The price then enters a mild corrective phase. This sets up the left shoulder. But, unlike what we saw in the continuation patterns of Chapter 7, the volume now starts to pick up during the correction. The corrective period ends soon, and investors used to buying on dips during the bull market start buying again fairly aggressively. After a spirited rally, the market rolls over again. At this point, only a few sense that the market has passed its cyclical peak. This is the head. But those few start selling with firm resolve, bailing out at what they believe is top dollar.

FIGURE 9-1

Ideal Head and Shoulders

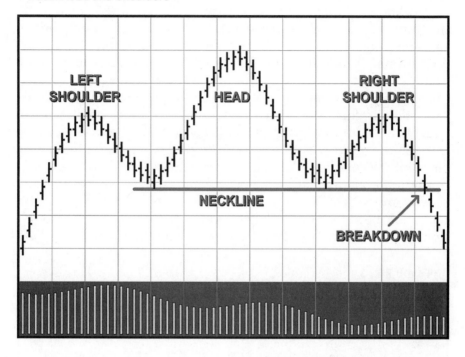

Once those initial profit takers have done their thing, the dip-buyers once again come to the fore. But surprise surprise, on this next rally the market does not achieve the level seen during the previous peak. This is the right shoulder. Does this guarantee that the bull market is over? Not necessarily. Such oddities can occur occasionally to interrupt a bull trend. But the thin volume of the rally should make us suspicious. The confirmation that the bull market is over comes when the price drives down through the level defined by the last trough that came before the ultimate peak. That price level is called the *neckline* in the head and shoulders analogy. It is drawn at the level where our imaginary person's neck meets the shoulders. When the price breaks down beneath this level, take cover. It is very likely that a bear market is in force.

The bear actually began growling the day after the highest peak. But market technicians could not have verified this until later price activity told them so. The first clue was the inability of the market to climb above the head during the right shoulder phase. The confirmation came as the price crashed through the neckline. This type of breakdown should be of great concern to anyone who still has the mind of a bull. Exiting the market at such a point may be the prudent thing to do. But far too many investors ignore such a sign and ultimately ride the new bear market all the way down to the bottom.

Figure 9-2 shows us a more realistic looking head and shoulders formation. In this case, the neckline is not quite horizontal, but it is nearly so. Note how, after the right shoulder, the price crashes through the neckline but rebounds the next day as bargain hunters come into the market believing they have found another dip-buying opportunity. Sadly, they were wrong, and the market resumes its downward course. When you see an obvious head and shoulders formation, head for the hills. Abandon your fond hopes for a resumption of the bull market. That may be a long time in coming. Take

FIGURE 9-2

Realistic Head and Shoulders

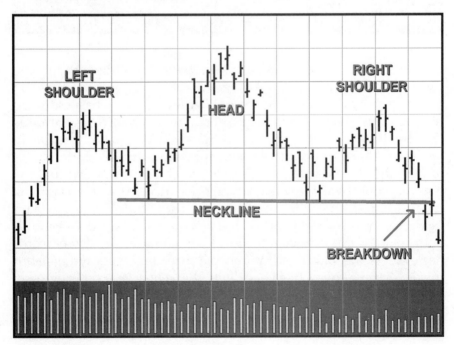

your profits, or accept your small losses, if that is what they are. Start
building up your cash for the time when the bull comes back.

DOUBLE TOP FORMATION

The head and shoulders formation that we just examined had a single primary peak with one minor peak on each side. Sometimes,
though, a pair of primary peaks can occur. This is seen in ideal form
in Figure 9-3, an example of a *double top formation*. It greatly resembles the head and shoulders formation, only it has two heads. We see
a powerful resistance line that contains the two heads. The lower
support line is quite similar to the neckline that we saw in the head
and shoulders formation. The center line, though, is a new feature
that adds quite a bit of complexity. Note that it alternates between
being a resistance line and a support line.

FIGURE 9-3

Ideal Double Top

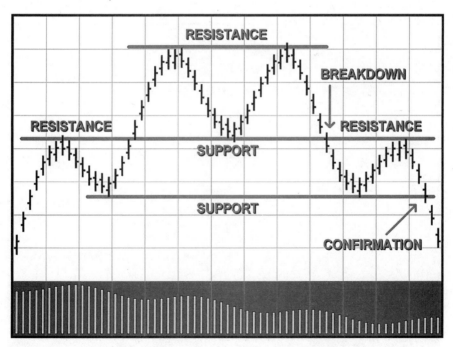

As with the head and shoulders formation, we see the continuation of an important bull trend in the left portion of Figure 9-3. Then the price starts to roll over into a corrective phase. The fact that volume picks up during this correction is not a good sign. But then the rally resumes and cares are forgotten. The next time that the market rolls over we note that it pulls back to match the point of an earlier peak. Thus, a resistance level shows an indication of transmuting into a support level. This is not at all unusual. Once the sellers had been cleared out at this level, buyers began to feel confident that at this price upward resistance would be minimal.

The problem comes when the next rally only matches the peak of the previous rally, creating the potential for a double top. That twin peak becomes a formidable resistance level. With volume picking up during pullbacks, bulls should start to consider abandoning their positions. When the price then crashes through what had become a support level, watch out. This is the point at which a breakdown is

F I G U R E 9-4

Realistic Double Top

indicated in Figure 9-3. Eventually, the price finds support at the same point it did many weeks earlier. This offers a glimmer of hope for those still believing in the bull market. But when the price only rallies back to our multipurpose line, concern should be great. When the market price drops through the lower support level, it's time to abandon all hope. The breakdown has been confirmed. The bear market has firmly entrenched itself. Those holding out for a return to record highs are deluding themselves if they think it will come any time soon. Much lower prices are in store for the stock or index represented by the chart.

Figure 9-4 demonstrates a double top formation in a more realistic manner. The support and resistance lines are not precisely horizontal, but the pattern should still be clear. The pattern of volume picking up during declines and faltering during advances should make the implications of the pattern all the more obvious.

Double tops occur fairly frequently, and their meaning should not be disregarded. Step aside when you recognize one. Maintaining hope could be hazardous to your wealth.

TRIPLE TOP FORMATION

More rarely seen than the head and shoulders formation or the double top formation is the *triple top formation*. But it does occur now and then, so it deserves some consideration. Actually, it is something of a cross between the head and shoulders and the double top. We see an idealized example in Figure 9-5. Instead of meeting important resistance twice, as with the double top, the price comes to this level three times. Perhaps the triple top formation even more closely resembles the head and shoulders, but with the head no higher than the shoulders.

The inability of the market price to punch through resistance three times is particularly disturbing. In the trading range channel, we notice that volume picks up no matter what the direction of the very short-term trend and cools off near the peaks and troughs. This indicates a great deal of hesitancy and indecision on the part of investors. That's a strong clue that the longer-term trend is about to be reversed. When, after three failed attempts to pierce upward resistance, the price then breaks down through support, get out of the way if you have not already. Notice the particularly limp rally attempt that comes after the breakdown.

FIGURE 9-5

Ideal Triple Top

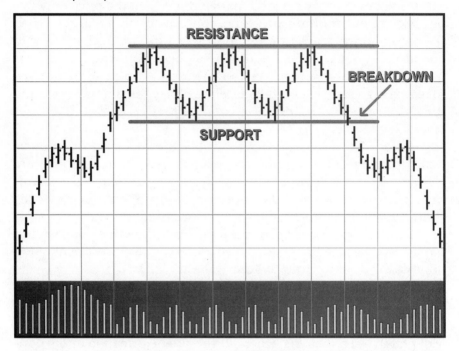

Figure 9-6 shows a more realistic example of a triple top formation. The pattern may not be as obvious as that seen in Figure 9-5, but the meaning is just as ominous. Do note how volume picks up during the early declines and lags during the rallies. Nevertheless, the overall volume trend is down as the market becomes a bear and investor interest wanes.

TOPPING FORMATIONS SUMMARY

Topping formations are the stop signs of the market. But just as an inattentive driver may drive through one, so will a complacent investor. It is so easy to be lulled into a false sense of security in the late phase of a bull market. The market has been moving up for quite a while. Sure, there have been occasional bouts of profit taking leading to minor corrections. But the buyers always seemed to come back, pushing stock prices to even higher plateaus. All the experts

FIGURE 9-6

Realistic Triple Top

tell you that this is a new era and the business cycle has been abolished. Your friends all have stories of huge profits and are eagerly anticipating ever more. But are they able to buy more shares? If not, cheerleading will not keep the market on an upward track.

The market reaches its peak at precisely the point at which the greatest number of investors believes that even greater profits lie ahead. That's the reason that prices are so high. As buyers keep demanding shares, potential sellers require higher prices before they will let go of their assets. But at the peak, a larger number of cautious investors start to exit the market. This is the distribution phase, in which more knowledgeable investors are unloading their shares at top dollar to the "greater fools," who are still all too eager to buy. This distribution phase can be detected in the topping formations that we have seen in this chapter. When you see these formations, do not wait to hear the news that explains the change in investor sentiment. Cash out and prepare for the next bull phase. We will be able to recognize that by the signs seen in Chapter 10.

10

BOTTOMING FORMATIONS

Time to Prepare Your Shopping List

A bear market is grueling. Your frustration may have caused you to exit the market at some point. If you were an alert technician, you may have been quick to recognize the topping formations discussed in Chapter 9 and averted much damage to your wealth. Others will have ridden the bear all the way down before waving the white flag and dumping their shares. The economic news is miserable, and few are interested in the market. It is precisely at this point that a few seasoned investors will start buying. This is the accumulation phase, and we can recognize it by using some of the charts we are about to study. It is a time for alertness, not apathy.

INVERTED HEAD AND SHOULDERS PATTERN

In Chapter 9 we learned about the head and shoulders pattern. That pattern provides us with an ominous warning. A much friendlier chap is one hanging by his feet. This is the *inverted head and shoulders pattern*. Figure 10-1 shows us an idealized example. On the left side, the bear is still pushing the market downward. We see one last failed rally attempt. But at the time we do not recognize it as the final failure. It is here that we are tracing out what we

FIGURE 10-1

Ideal Inverted Head and Shoulders

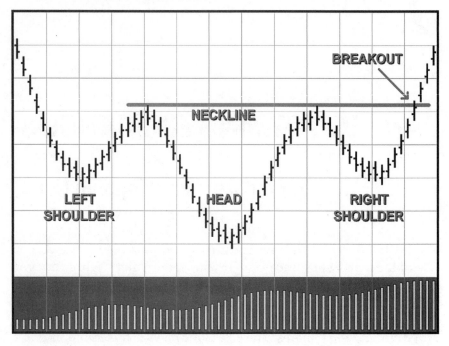

will eventually recognize as the left shoulder. The market than makes its ultimate bottom. This is the upside-down head. But we still do not have strong evidence that this is the ultimate bottom. The market starts to pick up then fails again. But this time something very interesting happens. Prices do not move down to meet the previous low. They only move to the level at which the market turned in the left shoulder. When the market then breaks through the resistance level (the neckline) that held back the market on either side of the head, we see a clear buy signal. Notice that as this entire pattern unfolds, the volume perks up during rallies and quiets down during corrections. This is confirmation that the market is going through an accumulation phase. The old bear is stepping aside for the baby bull.

Figure 10-2 shows us a more realistic version of an inverted head and shoulders formation. Nevertheless, the breakout should

FIGURE 10-2

Realistic Inverted Head and Shoulders

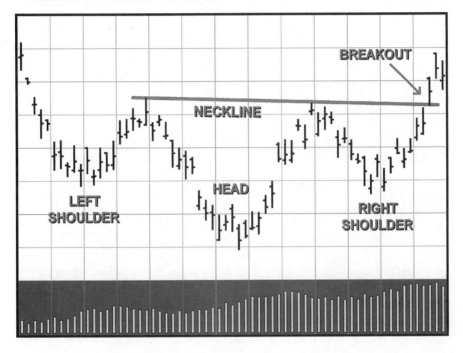

be obvious. Sometimes, the picture will be even more nebulous. But the more you trade using charts, the better experienced you will become at recognizing the opportunities represented by the inverted head and shoulders formation.

DOUBLE BOTTOM FORMATION

At other market bottoms, we may not see the classic single bottom of an inverted head and shoulders formation. Instead, we may witness what we see in Figure 10-3, a *double bottom formation*. This is, of course, an idealized example. But we must first picture the ideal in our minds before we can detect real-world examples. As we enter the pattern on the left, a bear market has been ongoing for some time. Each trough has been lower than the previous one. Then

Ideal Double Bottom

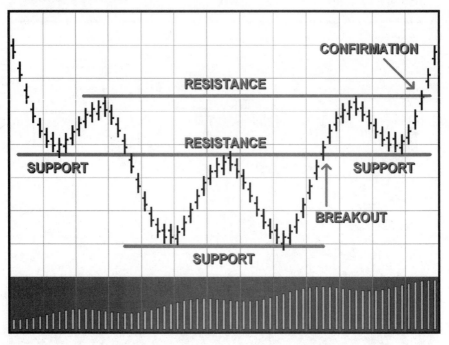

a curious thing happens. Another new trough holds at the level of the previous one. This is the double bottom. When the price then moves above the peak seen between the twin troughs, we see a breakout and the first buy signal. But it is still a time for only the more speculative investors to consider entering the market. If, after the next dip, the market quickly reverses and moves above the resistance met before entering the double bottom, we have confirmation that the breakout was genuine. This second buy signal is the time for conservative investors to start feeling more confident.

Figure 10-4 shows a more realistic looking double bottom formation. Notice that the double bottom formation is accompanied by a volume pattern similar to that of the inverted head and shoulders formation. We see increased activity during rallies and relative lack of interest during declines. This again is confirmation that the trend of the market has reversed from negative to positive.

FIGURE 10-4

Realistic Double Bottom

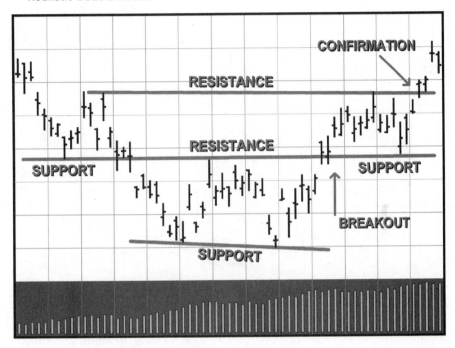

TRIPLE BOTTOM FORMATION

Just as triple top formations are relatively rare, so too are *triple bottom formations*. But they occur often enough to justify a look at Figure 10-5. They are similar to double bottom formations, but a little hitch occurs. After the second bottom, the ensuing rally is relatively weak. The price returns to the bottom for a third time before beginning the real advance. But once the market breaks above the resistance level that had already turned it back twice, we can feel better about the prospects for the future. Notice how, throughout the unfolding pattern, the volume perks up during rallies and lags during setbacks. And even more telling, the overall volume trend is up, indicating that the investor interest is picking up. That's a good sign that the bear is stepping aside for the bull.

Figure 10-6 is a more realistic version of a triple bottom formation. But all of the bullish signs are still there. Burn the ideal patterns into your mind, but be flexible enough to see them in less obvious circumstances.

FIGURE 10-5

Ideal Triple Bottom

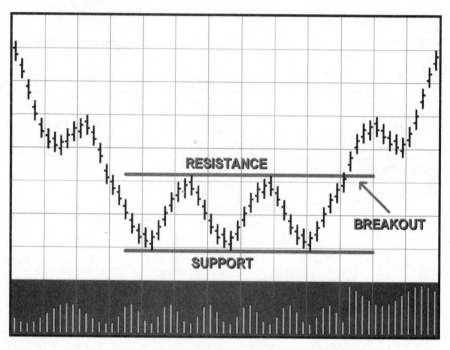

BOTTOMING FORMATIONS SUMMARY

As bottoms form, all of the news will be bad. It is a time when it's easy for an investor to be apathetic. Why not? Everyone else is. And that is indeed why prices are so low. Folks have become accustomed to a bear market and are determined not to throw good money after bad. Few have been buying; many have been selling. But for those determined to eventually make a profit in the market, this is the time to be alert for signs in the charts. Those technical signs will appear long before the economic news (for a company or the general market) starts to sweeten. The bottoming formations that we have examined in this chapter represent the accumulation phase. This is the time when savvy investors are paying bargain basement prices to those who are giving up. By paying attention to the charts when everyone else's attention is averted, you will be able to climb on

FIGURE 10-6

Realistic Triple Bottom

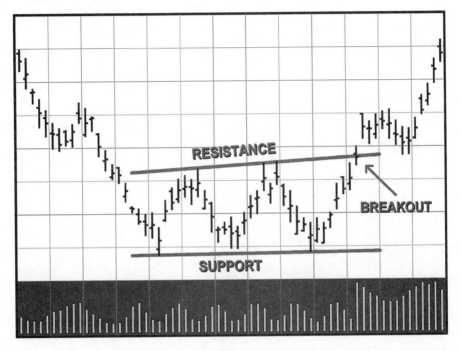

board the next bull market at an early stage, when prices are major bargains.

In Chapters 7 through 10, we have been looking at the most important classical technical patterns. In Chapter 11, we will learn to apply more confirming evidence of a pattern's validity. We will learn about *moving averages*.

11

THE CRYSTAL BALL

Using Moving Averages

In Chapters 7 through 10, we learned the basic technical patterns that tell us whether we are in a bull or a bear market. We also learned how to detect when we were in transition periods between the two. The patterns apply to both the general market averages and individual stocks. But are they perfectly reliable? Of course not. No one has yet developed a perfect system. Or, if someone has, he or she is not telling us. But the basic patterns do have a good track record when properly read and applied. A number of more complex patterns have been discerned, but they are beyond the scope of this primer. The ones covered in this book should apply to 95 percent of the situations that you might encounter. But there is a method for confirming your interpretation of a market, no matter which of the chart formations you believe that you are seeing. That method is *moving averages*.

Simple moving averages will be discussed in this chapter. There are a number of complex ways of weighting them, but I have found that the simplest is still the most useful.

To obtain a 10-day moving average, just examine the closing price of a stock or index for each day during a period of 10 trading days. Add up the 10 prices and divide the total by 10. Then plot this new value on a chart by placing it on the same day as the tenth closing price. In all probability, it will be a little higher or lower than the actual closing price, but it will be on the same vertical line. For the next day do the same thing. This process is simplified if you have a record of the 10-day total you had summed the day before. You subtract the first day and then add the new day. Then we connect the dots. And there it is: a 10-day moving average. Of course, this can be done for moving averages of various lengths. Commonly used periods are 10, 20, 50, and 200 days.

The technique of moving averages tends to smooth out the graph of a stock or index price. Unusual daily fluctuations seem to lose their importance. Trends and meaningful turning points may become more obvious.

A SINGLE MOVING AVERAGE

Moving averages are most informative when compared with the regular price chart. For long-term (6 months or more) investors, I find the 200-day moving average to be the most useful. Figure 11-1 again

FIGURE 11-1

Ideal Head and Shoulders with Moving Average

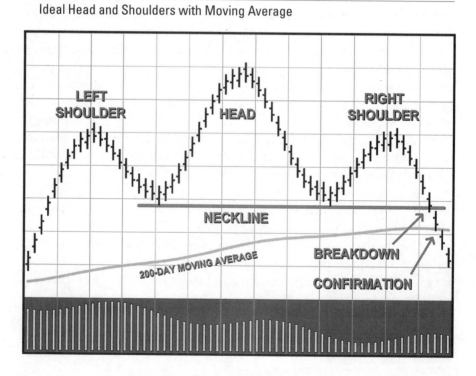

shows our old nemesis, the head and shoulders formation. But this time I have added the 200-day moving average. Throughout most of the chart, the price remains above the 200-day moving average. The general rule with moving averages is to assume that the trend will remain in place until the moving average is crossed by the actual price curve. When this particular chart began, our stock was in a bull phase. We learned in Chapter 9 on topping formations that a sell signal would be triggered when the price broke down through the neckline. In this example, we get confirmation only a day or two later when the price crashes through the 200-day moving average. Those who had doubts about the validity of the signal given in the head and shoulders formation can now feel more confident that the bear has arisen.

Figure 11-2 demonstrates the reverse situation. Here we bring back our friend the inverted head and shoulders pattern. As the tracing begins, the stock is in a bear market. And, as is usual in a bear market, the

FIGURE 11-2

Ideal Inverted Head and Shoulders with Moving Average

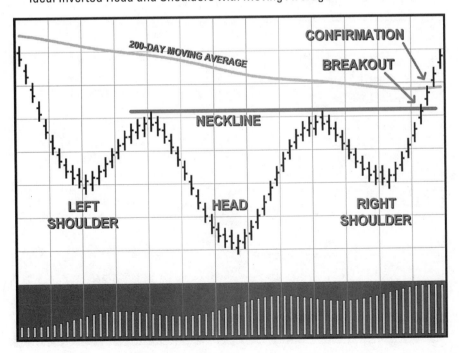

price remains below the 200-day moving average. But shortly after it breaks above the neckline, it also soars through the 200-day moving average. Thus, we get a buy signal and almost immediate confirmation of a new uptrend.

Of course, the previous examples used idealized price tracings that were almost as smooth as the moving averages. Figures 11-3 and 11-4 show more realistic situations. In these, the relative smoothness of the 200-day moving average is more obvious. But again, in both cases we see the 200-day moving average being breeched very shortly after the more basic technical signal was given.

The examples of 200-day moving averages given here were shown in conjunction with the two types of head and shoulders patterns. The 200-day moving average can be applied equally well to all of the basic technical patterns shown in this book. Breaking through the 200-day moving average will provide confirmation of your basic technical analysis.

FIGURE 11-3

Realistic Head and Shoulders with Moving Average

FIGURE 11-4

FIGURE 11-4

Realistic Inverted Head and Shoulders with Moving Average

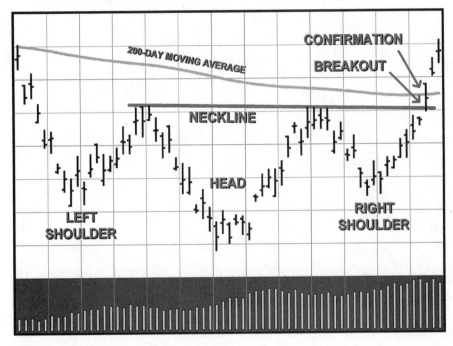

PAIRS OF MOVING AVERAGES

I've found that shorter period moving averages can be quite useful to the short-term trader when they are compared against one another. The juxtaposition of the 10-day and 20-day moving averages seems to work best for this purpose. Figure 11-5 shows a very simple topping formation: a *rounding top*. It may be the head of a very extended head and shoulders formation. More likely, it does not fit any of the previously discussed categories. That would make it difficult for the formation to indicate a good point for a sell signal. A pair of moving averages would be helpful. Note that the 10-day moving average hugs more closely to the true graph than the 20-day moving average. The sell signal is issued when the 10-day moving average crosses over the 20-day moving average. True, this misses the exact top. But that is the case in virtually all of our charts. We can, however, feel more confident that the change in trend is real at the point where the two moving averages cross.

FIGURE 11-5

Ideal Rounding Top with Two Moving Averages

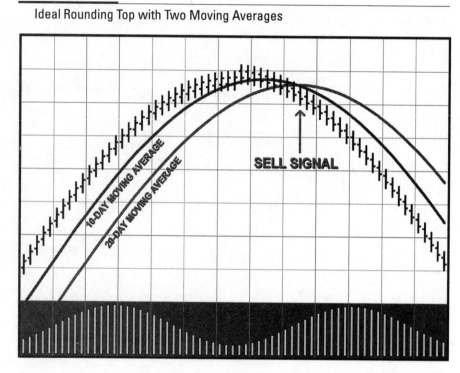

If we get out of the stock at this point, we will have saved almost all of our profit and will have little regret that we may be missing even greater near-term gains.

Figure 11-6 shows a similar example for an idealized bottoming formation. It appears to be a rounding bottom formation that offers little in the way of a clear-cut signal for a buy point. Again, a pair of moving averages comes to the rescue. We don't catch the exact bottom. But we can be more confident of the uptrend if we wait until the two moving averages cross.

Figures 11-7 and 11-8 show more realistic rounding top and rounding bottom formations. Despite their simplicity, these rounding formations are often the most difficult for a technician to interpret. This is because clear support and resistance lines are usually lacking. But when other methods fail, the moving averages come to the fore.

FIGURE 11-6

Ideal Rounding Bottom with Two Moving Averages

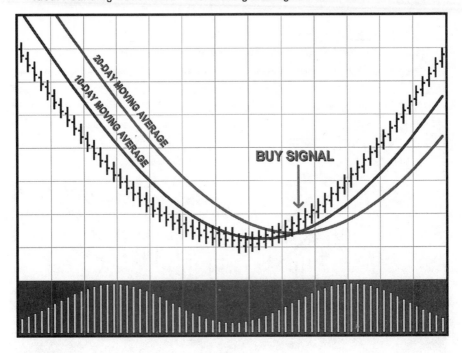

FIGURE 11-7

Realistic Rounding Top with Two Moving Averages

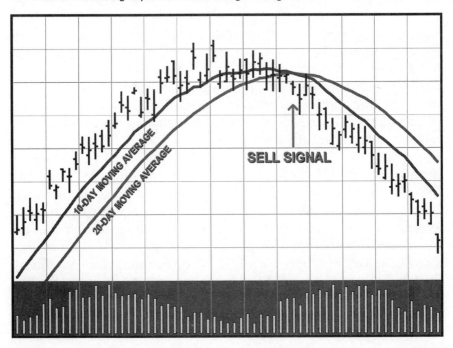

FIGURE 11-8

Realistic Rounding Bottom with Two Moving Averages

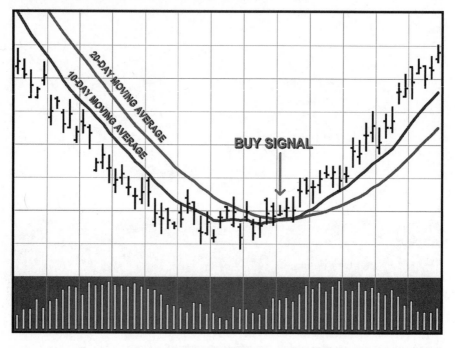

Figure 11-9 shows a choppy chart in which technical analysis may be difficult. But our moving averages save the day. During the fourth week of the chart, the 10-day moving average moves above the 20-day moving average. This is a good short-term buy signal confirming that a short-term bottom was set 2 weeks earlier. When the price bottomed during the second week, there may have been a temptation to get on board right away. Those who did profited handsomely. But it could have been a false bottom. More prudent investors would have waited for the confirmation from the moving averages. After 6 weeks, the price briefly dipped under the 10-day moving average. But it stayed above the 20-day moving average, and the two moving averages did not cross each other. This was an indication that the immediate dip was only temporary. But it was also a warning that a more important turndown might be forthcoming. Indeed, during the latter weeks of the chart, we see choppy price action and the two moving averages getting wrapped around each other. A short-term investor who bought at the week four buy signal, may have wanted

FIGURE 11-9

Choppy Market with Two Moving Averages Indicating a Buy Signal

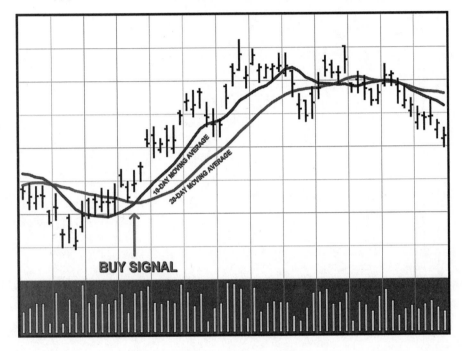

to consider exiting during this period of uncertainty. As it turned out, that would have been the right thing to do, as the price started a steady decline with the final crossing of the 10-day moving average beneath the 20-day moving average.

Figure 11-10 shows another choppy chart with few clear technical indications. The 10-day moving average is seen crossing under the 20-day moving average at the end of the third week. This presents a sell signal for the short-term trader. The wisdom of having taken action there may have been in doubt up until early in the sixth week. Up to that point, there had not been much of a decline, and the averages were threatening to cross in the opposite direction. But patience would have won out because the averages diverged even further as the price plummeted. At the right end of Figure 11-10, the market has again entered a choppy trading range and the averages are again threatening to cross. But prudence would ask one to wait until they actually do before entering a long position.

FIGURE 11-10

Choppy Market with Two Moving Averages Indicating a Sell Signal

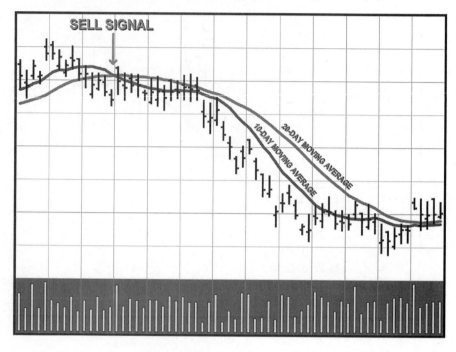

MOVING AVERAGE SUMMARY

Moving averages tend to smooth out price data and make market trends and meaningful turning points more obvious. For longer-term investors, the 200-day moving average is a very useful tool. It is generally correct to stay with a stock position so long as its price remains above the 200-day moving average. And it may not be wise to enter a long-term position until the price moves above its 200-day moving average. But this simple procedure works best as a complement to some of the more basic technical methods. Examining the 200-day moving average often confirms other technical indications.

Comparing two moving averages works especially well when used in conjunction with charts that may not have other technical clues. Rounding tops and bottoms are the most notable cases. Looking for crossing points between 10-day and 20-day moving averages may be particularly helpful for the short-term trader.

12

OTHER SYSTEMS

Oscillating Waves

The chart patterns that we have examined in this book are classic and have been used by a great many market technicians for nearly a century. Since then, many newer systems and theories have been developed. Once you have mastered the basics, you may want to make a detailed study of these methods. These newer methods were not meant to replace traditional technical analysis; they generally serve as complements. This book is a primer, and we will not be able to go into detail regarding these other methods. However, I will briefly describe some of them in this chapter so that you can decide for yourself if you want to pursue further study.

ARMS INDEX

The Arms Index or TRIN was already touched upon in Chapter 3. It was invented by Richard Arms back in the 1960s. Arms is a New Mexico–based money manager. His Web site is *www.armsinsider.com*. You can go to this Web site to learn more about the Arms Index and how to obtain such books as *The Arms Index*, *Profits in Volume*, and others. TRIN is the ticker symbol for the index on most quote machines. It stands for short-term trading index, which was the original designation. Later the inventor asked that it be called the Arms Index, and most investors have gladly complied.

The calculation for the Arms Index is not really that difficult, but many are put off when they hear that it is a ratio of ratios. Lots of people avoid mathematical concepts. But there is no higher math here, just simple division. The first ratio that must be calculated is obtained by dividing the day's advancing stocks on the New York Stock Exchange by the declining stocks. An advancing stock is one that is priced higher than the previous day's closing price. A declining stock is one that is priced lower than the previous day's closing price. The second ratio involves the volume going into these stocks. The volume going into the advancing issues is divided by the volume going into the declining issues. The final trick is to divide our first ratio by the second ratio. The result is the Arms Index. It neatly combines the concepts of price and volume that we have been emphasizing throughout this book.

An Arms Index reading of exactly 1.00 is neutral. A reading under 1.00 (it never gets under 0.00) indicates more volume going into each advancing issue than each declining issue. This is indicative of buying interest. A reading above 1.00 (no upside limit) indicates more volume going into each declining issue than each advancing issue. This shows selling pressure. The fact that low values represent buying interest and high values represent selling pressure is troublesome to many. They find it counterintuitive. Of course, if some of the required data had been switched, high numbers would show buying and low numbers would show selling. Arms once told me that he wished he had originally constructed the index in such a manner. But it became popular so quickly that it could not be changed.

The previous paragraph describes the immediate meaning of the Arms Index. But many technicians view the Arms Index in a manner contrary to this. If the Arms Index has been giving low readings for several days in a row and then closes near the low of the day with a reading under 0.50, that may seem bullish. It does point to a great deal of buying interest. But it may also indicate an overbought condition. Remember, the Arms Index itself tells us what *has* been happening, not necessarily what is going to *continue* to happen. A string of "good" readings may indicate that something "bad" is about to happen.

Conversely, if the Arms Index has been giving high readings for several days in a row and then closes near the high of the day with a reading over 2.00, that may seem bearish. Obviously, there has been a lot of selling pressure. But it can warn us of an oversold condition. Technicians who view the Arms Index in this manner are known as *contrarians*. They notice recent behavior and do not expect it to continue. Arms Index contrarians, though, are only looking at short-term possibilities.

THE MCCLELLAN OSCILLATOR

As we discussed in Chapter 3, Sherman McClellan and his wife Marian invented the *McClellan Oscillator* more than 30 years ago. Like the Arms Index, the McClellan Oscillator involves knowledge of the number of advancing issues and declining issues on the New York Stock Exchange. The difference (sometimes the ratio) between the two is something that we market technicians call *breadth*.

The McClellans then examined moving averages of advancing issues and declining issues. But not the simple moving averages we discussed earlier. Instead, they used two different exponential moving averages and compared them. The method for constructing the McClellan Oscillator is not as simple as the one for constructing the Arms Index. We invite the interested reader to go to *www.mcoscillator.com* for details.

Basically, if a McClellan Oscillator reading is positive, it points to money flowing into the market. If the value is negative, it shows money leaving the market. But, as with the Arms Index, extreme readings can indicate overbought and oversold conditions.

Tom McClellan, the son of Sherman and Marian McClellan, has also become heavily involved with technical analysis and the McClellan Oscillator. Tom's West Point education seems especially well suited to keeping an objective point of view. Both father and son produce biweekly newsletters that reflect their keen interpretations of the market. Tom also sends out a detailed daily edition after each market day. You would learn a lot about technical analysis if you followed Tom's daily treatise. Details on the McClellans' publications can be obtained at their Web site.

THE ELLIOTT WAVE

Back in the 1930s, Ralph Nelson Elliott suspected that there were natural patterns in the movements of stock prices. We discussed some natural patterns in Chapter 2. Some were related to seasonal factors. Some involved complex interactions that nevertheless resulted in predictable systems (remember the foxes and rabbits?). Elliott saw some of these patterns in nature and in the nature of human beings. He especially saw patterns of human mass psychology. Some of these patterns could last a very long time. This could result in the alternating high civilizations and dark ages we discussed earlier. At the shortest terms, this can be seen in erratic minute-to-minute jumps in stock price. But whether he was examining long-term, intermediate-term, or short-term price action, Elliott believed he saw similar patterns. When he placed longer-term patterns under a microscope, he saw smaller versions of the same pattern. Mathematicians call such relationships *fractals*.

Let's examine the simplest possible pattern of price movement. This is seen in Figure 12-1. It shows a simple bull phase in the market followed by a bear phase. As is normal, the bull phase runs about twice as long as the bear phase and produces a positive net effect.

FIGURE 12-1

Simplified Market Cycle

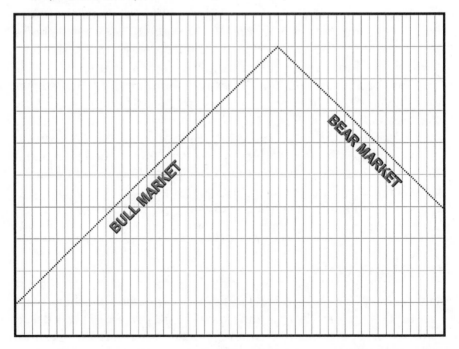

FIGURE 12-2

Basic Elliott Wave Cycle

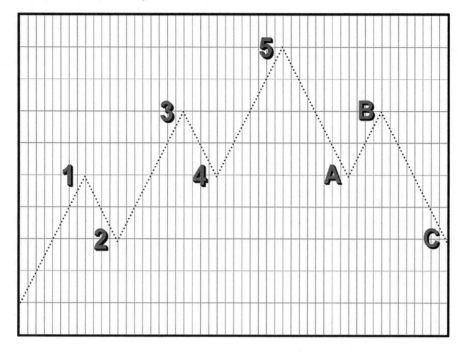

Figure 12-2, though, is more interesting. This encapsulates the basic Elliott concept. Notice that the previously seen bull phase is now divided into five "waves," as Elliott called them. The waves are labeled toward the end of each movement. The odd-numbered waves are rising, and the even-numbered waves are falling. But when we move into the bear phase, only three waves are noted. Waves A and C point downward, while wave B marks an intervening rally.

I mentioned that Elliott saw these patterns at all levels. Figure 12-3 is similar to Figure 12-2, but shows us even shorter-term patterns. The waves that we saw in Figure 12-2 are indicated by the larger numerals and letters. Examine the wave with the large numeral 1. In Figure 12-3, wave 1 is now divided into five waves that are smaller, but similar to, the entire bull phase. These five waves are labeled with smaller numbers. But note that the original wave 2 is divided into only three smaller waves denoted by smaller letters.

The manner in which the larger waves 1 and 2 subdivide denotes a greater principle. That principle is that a shorter-term

FIGURE 12-3

Ideal Complex Elliott Wave Cycle

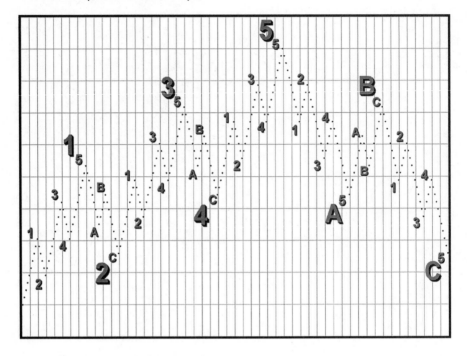

pattern moving in the same direction as the next longer-term pattern moves in five waves. But a shorter-term pattern moving counter to the next longer-term pattern is divided into only three waves. Five-wave patterns are labeled with numbers. Three-wave patterns are labeled with letters.

Examine the longer-term bear phase in the right third of Figure 12-3. Notice that the bear phase declines are divided into five waves, but the rally has only three waves. Again, this is in agreement with the concept that movements in the direction of the next larger trend are divided into five waves and those moving countertrend are divided into three waves. This is key. Smaller formations exhibiting three-wave patterns tell us that the price is moving contrary to the larger trend. Small five-wave patterns tell us that the market is moving in the same direction as the larger trend.

Figure 12-4 depicts a somewhat more realistic looking market pattern, but still with only daily closes as in Figure 12-3. But we

FIGURE 12-4

Realistic Complex Elliott Wave Cycle

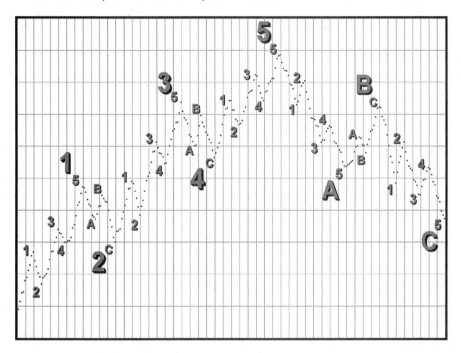

could examine hourly or minute-to-minute charts and still find patterns similar to those that Elliott saw. We could also examine much longer-term charts and find that Figure 12-4 serves as a small wave in a larger structure.

Unlike some of the alternative systems we discussed earlier, Elliott Wave analysis is more of an art than a science. In Chapter 14, we discuss how technical analysis can become intuitive. Intuitive skills are even more necessary for seeing Elliott Waves. Real world Elliott Waves can be even less obvious than those seen in Figure 12-4. As a result, different "Elliotticians" will see different patterns in a stock chart and will come to different conclusions.

Robert Prechter is the individual most noted for the study and application of Elliott Wave analysis. A quarter century ago, Prechter and A. J. Frost wrote *The Elliott Wave Principle*. Prechter publishes the monthly *Elliott Wave Theorist*. His most recent book is *Conquer the Crash*. He was greatly celebrated back in the 1980s as he called for a new and powerful long-term bull market when most everyone else was content with high-yielding money market funds. He also warned of a great bear market to follow, although it may have come a little later than he originally expected. You can learn more about Elliott Wave analysis and Prechter's publications by going to *www.elliottwave.com*.

Practicalities

13

MUTUAL FUND SWITCHING AND STOCK TIMING

It's Your 401(k)—Run It!

In times past, many workers were promised specific pension payouts after their retirement. To fund these benefits, companies would invest in safe conservative investments. That, of course, meant modest but relatively certain returns. During the bull market of the 1980s and 1990s, many workers demanded and received the right to invest their pension funds as they saw fit. Enter the 401(k) plan.

During the transition to 401(k) plans, workers were asked to attend meetings presided over by an agent representing the family of mutual funds that would be managing the pension money. Workers were told that they would have to allocate various percentages of their 401(k) assets into their choices of funds within the fund family. They would be provided with some advice on which funds to choose based on their individual ages and risk tolerances. But the ultimate decision was each person's own. Participants in 401(k) plans were generally told that they could change their allocations at any time, even on a daily basis. For most of these changes, there would be no commissions or penalties. However, a few select funds did have withdrawal penalties if a position was not held for a minimum period of time. The employees were advised not to switch frequently. They were told to avoid switching because it was folly to try to time the market. And for most people, that is indeed true. As was expressed earlier in this book, most folks will invest with their emotions. They will buy at market peaks and sell at market troughs. Perhaps the mutual fund agent did not mention the fact that frequent switching can be a costly headache for the fund managers.

Many of these 401(k) programs were set up right at the peak of the market around the turn of the millennium. Naturally, that was just when there was the most demand from employees for control of their own pension money. They felt they were missing out on a great bull market as the company invested their funds conservatively. So the companies obliged them. Why not? Defined benefits programs were a huge obligation. In many cases, a firm's pension costs were reduced if it simply supported 401(k) plans.

In Chapter 3, we learned what happens when everyone gets on the same side of the boat. With the implementation of 401(k) plans the general public moved its pension money into the stock market. That should have been an alarm signal. It indicated that all willing money was now in stocks. That was a setup with a lot more potential sellers than buyers. The completion of this transition to 401(k) plans should have been viewed by a contrarian as a sign of a potential market peak. And, indeed, that is the way it turned out. The market then turned over and tanked for years. But most of those new 401(k) participants did as they were told. They stuck with their positions and watched huge chunks of their retirement money evaporate.

But should a good market technician, who also happens to be a 401(k) participant, resist changing his or her fund allocation? No, not if he or she is really good at it. Good technicians saw the bubble burst in 2000 and switched to money market funds before stock prices had contracted very much. Not so good ones (usually those who let their hearts do their charting for them) rode their growth funds down to the ground along with most everyone else.

Many who lost money blame the mutual fund managers. For the most part, it was not really any one manager's fault. Not unless the fund was one in which the manger had a great deal of discretion as to how much to put into stocks, bonds, or cash. In most cases, the manager is required by the fund's prospectus to keep virtually all of the fund's assets in a certain class of investments. The ability to switch funds puts most of the onus on the owner of the 401(k) fund to decide when to be in cash and when to be elsewhere.

If you think that you are a good enough technician to frequently switch your pension funds from one mutual fund to another, then test your ability first. Chart all the funds in your mutual fund family into which you might consider making investments. Daily prices for the funds will generally be reported on your fund family's Web site. If you prefer to read newspapers, then ask your fund family where the funds are listed and under what symbols.

It was earlier stated that the charting techniques in this book apply equally well to individual stocks and to stock indices. They also work well with an industry group. And they can be applied to mutual funds. The drawback is a lack of volume data. Nevertheless, charting the funds would be a fine way to begin honing your skills as a technician.

After you have charted at least a month's worth of fund prices, get out your ruler. Start drawing out the support and resistance levels. See if you can recognize any of the patterns discussed earlier in this book. Then make a note of your prediction of how the pattern will unfold in the future. Later, be sure to note how your predictions pan out.

Were your predictions correct a few times? Don't get too excited. They may have been happy coincidences. Keep working at your charting practice until you are right a large majority of the time.

Once you have achieved a great deal of confidence in your ability to apply technical analysis to mutual fund charts, it still may be wise to be slow to pull the trigger. Funds will generally be slower to make turns than individual stocks. It is usually prudent to wait a little longer to make switches in the fund arena. It may be wise to wait for additional confirming indicators. Moving averages, especially the 200-day moving average, could be very helpful. An uptrend is likely to remain intact as long as the fund price remains above its 200-day moving average. And a downtrend will probably continue to prevail while the fund price stays under its 200-day moving average. But once a new trend has become established, and you believe there is sufficient technical confirmation, then do consider switching your allocation.

STOCK TIMING

Chart and Grow Rich

The techniques presented in this book work well for stock indices, industry sectors, and commodities such as gold, corn, and crude oil.

But perhaps their most useful application for most individual investors is with individual stocks.

A mutual fund manager is virtually compelled to own a large number of different companies. He or she cannot or will not take the risk of being concentrated in too few stocks. Even if he or she were in the right ones, the transaction costs of getting in and out of very large positions would be too high. A technically minded money manager will study the charts of major indices such as the Standard & Poor's 500. But he or she may rely on the fundamentals for the individual stock selection. This puts you at an advantage.

The individual investor will normally have far fewer stocks in his or her portfolio than a money manager—perhaps only 5 to 10, maybe 20. And the quantities held are smaller. This gives you more flexibility. And in your own self-interest, you may be willing to chart each stock you own or are considering buying. You are strongly encouraged to do so.

Yes, you can subscribe to charting services such as DecisionPoint.com and StockCharts.com. Eventually you may want to do so. But you owe it to yourself to do your own busywork at first. Doing so will give you a far deeper understanding of technical analysis. It will also give you a better feeling for the price tendencies of companies that you own.

You may want to first chart the stocks that you already own. Try to prepare a chart for each one. Each day you can retrieve the prices from a newspaper or off the Internet. Your brokerage can provide such information. For each stock on a separate chart, plot the day's high, low, open, and close. Underneath, plot each day's trading volume.

Once you have at least a month's worth of data, get out your ruler. Start with your favorite stock holding. Is there an obvious zone of support? That is a price level that seems to stem declines and bring in buying interest. If so, draw a horizontal line at that level and label it *support*. If not, then note each short-term trough. Is it possible to connect several bottoms with a nearly straight line? Then do so. You have now established a support line. Beneath this line lies a group of willing buyers who feel that the stock is a bargain at this level. They have proven their willingness and ability to enter the market at this price. If the support line is horizontal, then expect the market not to make any progress either way for a while. If it is up-sloping, then expect the bullish trend to remain intact. If it is down-sloping, then we will need to look extra carefully at the resistance line that we will soon be drawing. If any of these lines are broken, especially on increased volume, then look for some important changes in stock price.

Now find your resistance line. Look for a level at which owners of the stock have proven their willingness to take profits. If it exists, draw a horizontal line. If not, then note each short-term peak. If possible, connect a series of peaks with a nearly straight line. This is your *resistance line*. If it is horizontal, the price may be contained by this limit for some time. If the resistance line is down-sloping, then a bearish trend may remain for a while. If it is up-sloping, then much depends on the direction of the support line and the direction of the market before this channel was established.

Once you have the chart before you with support and resistance lines drawn in, try to determine which of the basic technical patterns it most resembles. You will find these patterns in Chapters 7 through 10 of this book. Does the volume pattern also seem to agree with the archetype? If you have a good candidate pattern, then make a prediction of the future price movement. Do this for each of the stocks that you are following. Each day as you add data to your charts, determine if your original predictions still seem valid. If one seems not to be, perhaps a different one of the basic technical patterns is actually a better match. If a solid majority of your predictions turn out to be correct, pat yourself on the back. You may be a budding technician. If not, then keep working at it. It may take a little sweat before the process becomes intuitive. That's a process we will be discussing in Chapter 14.

You may want to hold off on taking action on your predictions until you are fully confident in your abilities as a market technician. A few lucky guesses may prematurely cause you to believe that you are a natural expert. If you do not seem to be able to get the hang of it and are not willing to continue developing your skills, at least you will have a gained a good understanding of what good market technicians are discussing when you listen to their analyses. And reading this book should have helped you to avoid the common mistakes that the rest of the crowd often makes.

14

FINAL EXAM

Diploma Time

MAKING IT SEEM EASY
When It All Becomes Intuitive

Learning to ride a bicycle began as a difficult and awkward experience. You had to be thinking constantly about everything involved. You had to be ever alert, as injury could result from any misstep. Eventually, of course, the procedure became intuitive. Even if you have not ridden a bike for years, you could get on one today and not think twice about the mechanics of keeping your balance. It can be the same with technical analysis. With sufficient practice, you should intuitively know what type of chart a stock is tracing out, even without drawing in the support and resistance lines. And you should more often than not be able to correctly predict the future direction of the price action. But getting to that stage requires practice, practice, practice. Just as it did when you learned to ride a bike.

Until it all becomes intuitive for you, keep drawing those charts by hand. If you try to learn technical analysis just by looking and not doing, you will never achieve the same level of instinct that you did with the bicycle. Would simply having read a book about bike riding done the job for you? Of course not. And it's the same way with technical analysis.

If you haven't spent enough time with technical analysis for it to become intuitive, you will doubtlessly fall back on those old instincts that did you in before. Fear and greed will again become the forces that propel your investment thinking. And that will be just as disastrous for your financial health as it was in the past.

If you are able to shed the costly habits of your past and look at the investment world with a more sober eye, your finances will likely be more in order. You will come to love the stock market rather than despise it. Like the child it is, it will occasionally get out of hand. But if proper attention is paid to it, you will be rewarded.

Eventually, you should be able to see a chart of stock prices—one that you have not drawn yourself—and be able to get a sense of what is to come. By then, you may not even have to draw the support and resistance lines. They will be seen by your mind's eye. This is the level to which you should aspire.

I have said before that you may not know the reason for a stock or the market to be moving in a certain direction. But your reading of the charts tells you that somebody must know something. Once you become skilled enough, you may even be able to correctly guess the reason fairly regularly. You will have seen the market move in your estimated direction and then the news will be broadcast that explains why. Perhaps it was a favorable earnings report. Perhaps it was a new invention or new product. Some purist technical analysts say they do not want to know. They say they do not even want to know the name of a company or what it does. They just want to see the chart. I prefer, however, to know something about a company's fundamentals. The charts are sometimes showing only hysteria and not the underlying business strength. Knowing more about the company itself may tell you which scenario is more likely. In the late 1990s, too many investors were totally unconcerned about a new company's business plan. They merely saw all the dot-coms soaring upward in price. It was smart to ride with those folks for a while. But poor fundamentals would have encouraged good technicians to look even more closely at the technicals than they might have in other circumstances. Those technicians would have seen a crash coming and gotten out when everyone else was still cheering.

Yes, with a honed intuitive instinct for the market, you may amaze everyone when you forecast what's going to happen before it happens. Will you be able to do this every time? Hardly. And many will never attain this ability. But with this book you have been given the basic tools. If you really become skilled at technical analysis, you may want to consult more advanced texts. You have been warned of the mistakes that investors too often make. At the very least, this book will have protected you from those errors.

Before you start the charting program suggested here, and long before you invest money based on your analysis, try your hand at the exercises that follow. Each problem will show you a stock chart that has not been fully traced out. Support and resistance lines will not have been drawn. But you should be able to do well, especially if you have read all the earlier chapters. Why shouldn't you? The charts are based on the same ones you came across earlier in this book.

TEST CHARTS
Now It's Your Turn

Most people do not like being tested. But you are the only one who will know the results of the tests in this chapter. And it is important that you do know those results. If you do not do well, it will be imperative that you review what you may have overlooked. Even if you have trouble with just a few of the test charts, you will want to review the chapters in which they were first introduced.

If you do well the first time, or after the fifth time, you will then want to start plotting the charts of stocks in which you have personal interest. You only want to make imaginary investments on paper to learn if you have really gotten the knack. If you never seem to get the knack, then consult professional technicians. At the very least, you will understand the language they are using and the reasoning behind their analyses.

As was explained earlier, the test charts are similar to the charts that you saw earlier in this book. All that is seen, however, are plots of the daily prices and accompanying volume activity. Support and resistance lines and other clues to market direction have been left out. It is up to you to draw those items that you need for guidance. First, pull back and get a good overall view of the chart. Try to get a feeling for the sweep of the price movement. Do you see patterns that you have seen before? Get out your straightedge. See if you can draw support and resistance lines. These may be horizontal, up-sloping, or down-sloping. They should connect areas where the market has turned in the past. The support lines are the points at which buyers have proven that they are willing to get on board. The resistance lines show us the levels at which willing sellers are likely to emerge. Look carefully at the volume. Determine when the volume is supporting a price move and when it is not.

A few days at the right end of each chart have been left off intentionally. It is here that you should note your prediction of future price movement. Following your test chart will be another chart similar to one seen earlier in the book. This chart will have all of the necessary lines drawn in and will show the price continuation for the final days. Do your drawing and prediction show agreement with the completed chart? If so, pat yourself on the back. But whether you got it right or not, check to see if your reasoning is in line with the accompanying commentary.

The odd numbered figures in this chapter show only the price and volume. Some of the days on the right side of the charts are also left out. It's your job to fill in the support and resistance lines and to determine the future price direction.

PROBLEM 1

Figure 14-1 is a classic. First look at the overall pattern. Then try to
determine where support and resistance lie. Make note of the volume
pattern. Then determine the future direction of the market. Try to
give the pattern a name if you can. This is the procedure that you will
follow with all of the problems in this chapter.

FIGURE 14-1

Problem 1

SOLUTION 1

Figure 14-2 fills in the blanks on Figure 14-1. Some would call this a W pattern. I prefer to call it a double bottom formation. The W is what you see, but the name imparts more meaning. We see strong resistance near the top of the chart and strong support near the bottom. In the middle we see a line that provides both support and resistance, depending on where we are in the price evolution. Breaking above that middle line after twice bouncing off lower support gives us a buy signal. Then, eventually finding support at what had been a resistance level and breaking through a higher resistance level only confirms our prediction that this stock will be moving substantially higher. The volume pattern also confirms this with lessening interest during declines and growing interest during rallies. And that growing interest is the general trend throughout the chart.

FIGURE 14-2

Solution 1

PROBLEM 2

Figure 14-3 displays some similarities to those seen in Problem 1.
But what's the big difference? Decide after doing the busywork.

FIGURE 14-3

Problem 2

SOLUTION 2

Figure 14-4 shows the markings of a classic double top formation. Some would call it an M pattern, because that is what it looks like. But double top formation is a more descriptive and ominous term. If you see one of these, watch out. The market is headed into decline. As with Problem 1, we see low-level support and high-level resistance. We also see a central line that provides both support and resistance. But twice in succession the upper resistance line turns the market back. And the lower support line ultimately fails. The first breakdown occurs at that hybrid line. Those who are early to jump get out here. But even buy-and-hold investors should consider leaving when the lower resistance line is broken. And the volume shows that selling pressure prevails throughout. Ultimately, the volume withers away, a sign of a new bear market.

FIGURE 14-4

Solution 2

PROBLEM 3

Figure 14-5 shows a somewhat erratic pattern that may not be well defined by any of the classic technical formations. Yet trends can be detected—and trends within trends. What should that tell you?

FIGURE 14-5

Problem 3

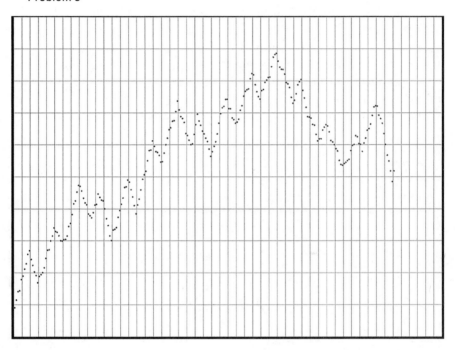

SOLUTION 3

If you tried to draw traditional support and resistance lines you may have detected two trends. You would have seen a bull market for the first two-thirds of the chart and then a bear market. We see no double or triple tops, although you may have discerned head and shoulders formations of different sizes. You get an A− if you called Figure 14-5 a head and shoulders formation. You would basically be right. But what you really wanted to notice here were the patterns within patterns. Mathematicians call these *fractals* when the smaller patterns resemble the larger patterns. Figure 14-6 makes clearer what we were looking for: a classic Elliott Wave pattern. Now we see the five wave movements going with the larger trend and the three wave movements when going countertrend. The more you work with technical analysis, the more you will be seeing Elliott Waves, even when more classic technical patterns are also apparent.

FIGURE 14-6

Solution 3

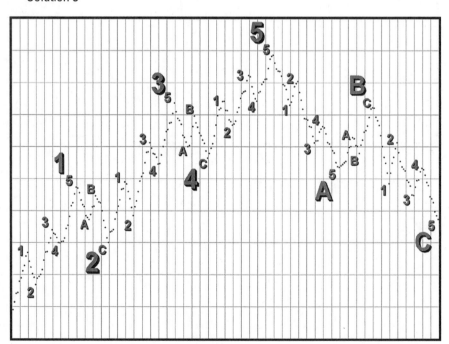

PROBLEM 4

Figure 14-7 demonstrates a rather common general occurrence. We see a trending market move into a trading range. But examine the price and volume carefully to determine future price action.

FIGURE 14-7

Problem 4

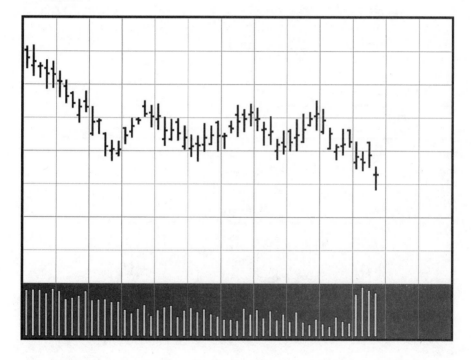

SOLUTION 4

Figure 14-8 has the support and resistance lines drawn, thus defining the channel for the trading range. The parallel lines are remi-
niscent of a flag formation. In this case it is a bearish flag formation.
The trend was obviously down before we entered the flag. So we
have an upside-down flagpole. The expectation is that the price will
eventually leave the flag to the downside. But we needed confirmation that this would be true. It could have been a triple bottom.
However, when the price breaks down on heavy volume when it
touches support for the fourth time, that is an ominous announcement that the bear has reawakened.

FIGURE 14-8

Solution 4

PROBLEM 5

Figure 14-9 bears some similarities to Problem 4. But its meaning is quite different. What can you discern?

FIGURE 14-9

Problem 5

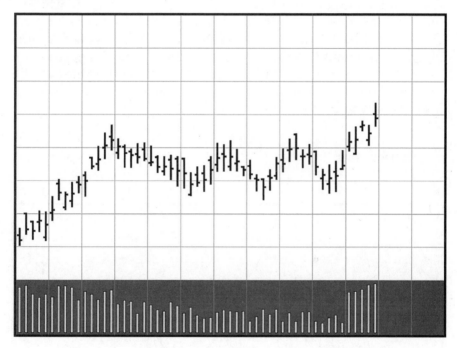

SOLUTION 5

Figure 14-10 shows that we are in one of the happiest formations of all. It is a bullish flag formation. It occurs quite frequently during a bull market. To the left of the chart we see a strong bull trend. Then we enter a consolidation phase. That's all it is. Usually it's nothing to be overly concerned about. But we must be cautious. There is the potential for a double or triple top here. The slight down-slopes to the parallel support and resistance lines are not particularly disturbing. Such slopes are often the case with a bullish flag formation. To the right, we see the classic flagpole. Then the waving flag during the trading range. When we see a breakout above the resistance line on heavy volume, we have increased confidence that the bull still prevails. Look for the next move up to at least equal the move seen during the flagpole.

F I G U R E   14-10

Solution 5

PROBLEM 6

Figure 14-11 should jump right out and grab you. Even a nontechnician should be able to tell you what it is.

F I G U R E   14-11

Problem 6

SOLUTION 6

There it is in Figure 14-12. The good old, bad old head and shoulders pattern. It appears frequently at market turns and brings with it an ominous warning. It tells us that the bull market has run its course. It shows one last hurrah and then peters out. The two shoulders and the head are standouts. The human mind has evolved to see human figures in almost everything. And another person is what most people see when viewing a chart like this. Once we draw in a neckline we know where the danger point is. If the market had kept going upward instead of forming a right shoulder, we may simply have been in a transitory bullish flag formation. Instead we broke down. The generally declining volume trend tells us that interest in the market has been waning. The fact that volume picked up a bit during the breakdown should not be heartening. The volume will likely rejoin the price in a downtrend.

FIGURE 14-12

Solution 6

PROBLEM 7

If you solved the last problem, then you should also know what
Figure 14-13 represents.

F I G U R E 14-13

Problem 7

SOLUTION 7

Figure 14-14 makes it clear that we are seeing an inverted head and shoulders pattern. This pattern often appears at the transition from a bear market to a bull market. It should be one of the most welcome patterns of all. However, conservative investors rarely recognize it. Yet they are the ones who should be alert for the next long-term opportunity. But they finally became frustrated with the bear market, if not during the left shoulder phase, then they joined the total capitulation crowd as the head was forming. The slowly rising volume trend gives a clue that savvy investors have started to accumulate shares. They have wisely been buying them from those who rode the market down and are now willing to get out at any price. When the decline to the right shoulder held well above the head and near the level of the left shoulder, investors should have been heartened. When the price broke above earlier resistance, the neckline, that should have been the all-clear signal for a new bull market.

FIGURE 14-14

Solution 7

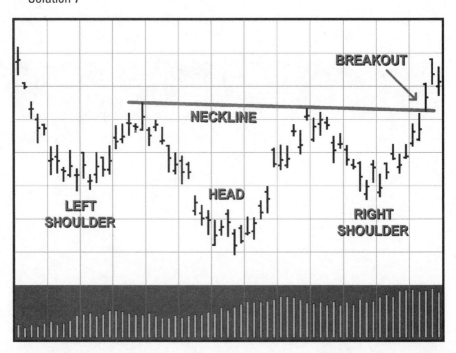

PROBLEM 8

Figure 14-15 illustrates a situation that has trapped many. Are you one of them?

FIGURE 14-15

Problem 8

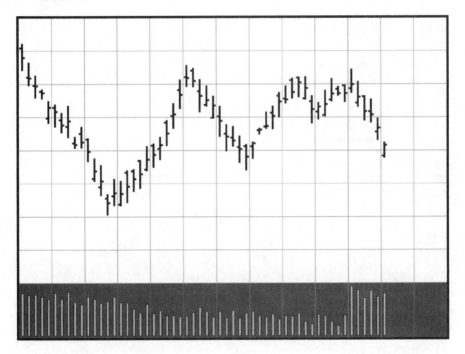

SOLUTION 8

The overly optimistic investor might have been fooled by that
uptrending support line. But the nearly horizontal resistance line
should have made you cautious. Figure 14-16 shows the pattern for
a bearish pennant formation. This is similar to the bearish flag formation. The difference is that during the trading range the buyers
keep getting braver but the bears just keep selling near the same
level they always had. Eventually the two groups come together,
and one has to give. When the price breaks though the support level
on heavy volume, that's a sign that some disturbing information is
filtering through the market and the bulls are the ones who are getting out of the way. You should too.

FIGURE 14-16

Solution 8

PROBLEM 9

Figure 14-17 shows some similarities to Problem 8. What are they?
What are the differences?

FIGURE 14-17

Problem 9

SOLUTION 9

Figure 14-18 demonstrates the reverse of what we saw in Problem 8. This is a bullish pennant formation. No matter how much the bears kept trying to sell, the bulls were always there at the support line. When the two camps came together, it was the bears who ran out of supply. The price then shot above the resistance line on heavy volume, indicating that the bull trend had resumed.

FIGURE 14-18

Solution 9

PROBLEM 10

Figure 14-19 might be a fooler. Don't let it be. It could be a form of a pattern that we have already seen in these tests. But it is not.

FIGURE 14-19

Problem 10

SOLUTION 10

It might have been a bearish flag formation. But it is not. Figure 14-20
demonstrates that we have been looking at a triple bottom formation,
a happy sign indeed. After three successful tests of support, the price
breaks above what had twice been resistance and exhibits heavy volume. Actually, the triple bottom formation shares many similarities
with the inverted head and shoulders pattern. The difference is that
the head extends no lower than the shoulders. In both cases, though,
a sustained bull phase usually follows.

FIGURE 14-20

Solution 10

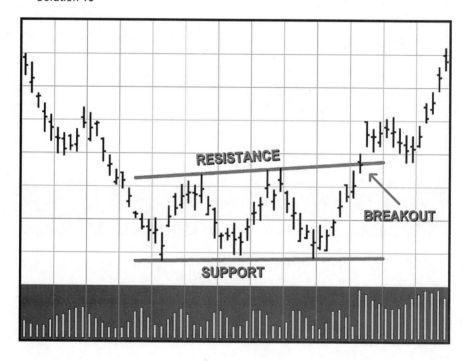

PROBLEM 11

Figure 14-21 shares some similarities with Problem 10. But its ultimate resolution is quite different.

F I G U R E 14-21

Problem 11

SOLUTION 11

In Figure 14-22, we see the contours of a classic triple top formation. It is not all that common, but it appears more often than a triple bottom formation. At first it might have appeared to be a bullish flag formation. However, when the price broke down through support it was evident that this was not the case. It is very similar to a head and shoulders pattern though. The difference is the diminished size of the head. Nevertheless, the implications are just as ominous as with the head and shoulders formation. Expect the baby bear cub to grow into a big old grizzly.

F I G U R E 14-22

Solution 11

PROBLEM 12

We may be drawing a fine line here. But Figure 14-23 is slightly different from a couple of other patterns in this test. However, its
meaning is similar. What is that?

F I G U R E 14-23

Problem 12

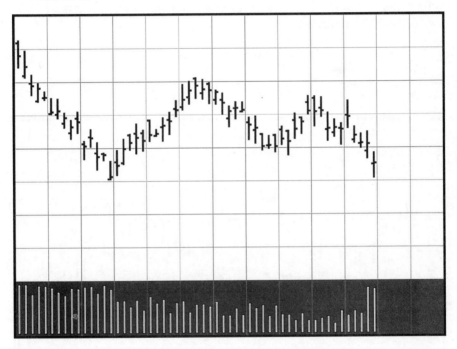

SOLUTION 12

In Figure 14-24, we see a bearish wedge formation. The price had
been trending downward until entering a trading range. The top
and bottom of this range both drew together over time. When the two
met, something was bound to give. Either the bears would run out
of supply or the bulls would run out of interest. In this case, the bulls
gave up. The price broke beneath the support line. Perhaps bad news
was forthcoming and somebody sensed it. That may have led to the
withdrawal of bids. In any event, "Katy bar the door." The bear market is likely to resume.

FIGURE 14-24

Solution 12

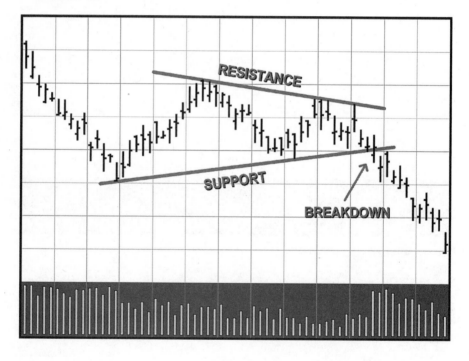

PROBLEM 13

Our last problem is seen in Figure 14-25. It is not at all unusual. What are you seeing? What does it foretell?

FIGURE 14-25

Problem 13

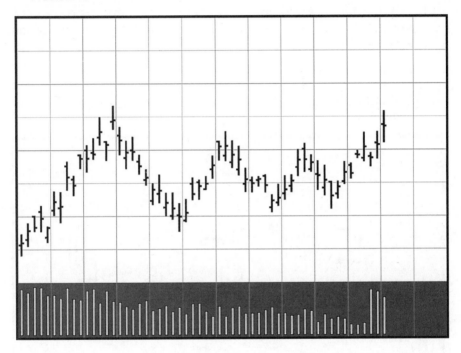

SOLUTION 13

This time we see the highlights of a bullish wedge formation in
Figure 14-26. We might have gotten worried as the bulls and bears
battled it out with support and resistance lines drawing ever closer
together. The softening volume may have been disheartening to a
bull, but this is not unusual as the amplitude of the trading range
diminishes. Finally, it is the bears that stop supplying shares, and
the market leaps forward on increased volume. Perhaps rumors of
good news have begun circulating. In any event, the bull trend has
resumed, and all is well.

F I G U R E 14-26

Solution 13

TEST CONCLUSION

Thirteen tests. No, this is not an unlucky number. It's just a *Fibonacci number*. What are those? Numbers like 2, 3, 5, 8, 13, and 21 are examples. They crop up frequently in the study of cycles and other phenomena. They are related to the golden ratio, 0.618, that we discussed earlier. Each adjacent pair forms a ratio that is closer to the golden ratio. If you would like to know more about Fibonacci numbers and how they are related to the market, then get a copy of Frost and Prechter's *Elliott Wave Principle*. In my case, I've been partial to the number 13 ever since I was lucky enough to hit four home runs and become the winning pitcher of a Little League game one Friday the thirteenth.

Did you hit home runs when you did the test problems? If so, congratulations! If not, do not despair. Was there something in particular that you seemed to miss? Were the support or resistance lines not evident? Did you forget to get clues from the volume? Spend time reviewing the tests you found most difficult.

You may or you may not become a proficient technical analyst. But this book should have helped you to understand the language of professional technical analysts, allowing you to comprehend more of what they say. And more important, the case that was built for technical analysis in the early chapters should make you a more aware investor. If nothing else, I hope this book has taught you to use only your objective head when making investment decisions. Save your heart for matters of romance.

INDEX

About the Author

Curt Renz is CEO of Curt Renz Capital Resources and the market strategist for CurtRenz.com. A former stockbroker, he was anchor and market analyst for *WebFN* and WCIU-TV in Chicago from 1987 to 2003.